Thomas Merton

Seeking Paradise

THE SPIRIT OF THE SHAKERS

Thomas Merton

 # Seeking Paradise

THE SPIRIT OF THE SHAKERS

Edited with an Introduction by Paul M. Pearson

ORBIS BOOKS
Maryknoll, New York

Published by Orbis Books, Maryknoll, NY 10545-0308.

Manufactured in the United States of America

Design: Roberta Savage

Library of Congress Cataloging-in-Publication Data

Merton, Thomas, 1915-1968.
   [Selections. 2003]
   Seeking paradise : the spirit of the Shakers / Thomas Merton ;
  edited with an introduction by Paul M. Pearson.
     p. cm.
   Includes bibliographical references.
   ISBN 1-57075-501-9 (pbk.)
   1. Shakers.   I. Pearson, Paul M. II. Title.
BX9772.M47 2003
289'.8—dc21

200300984

*This book is dedicated to
my father, Albert Pearson (1922-1998),
and to Anne, the grandaughter he never met.
May the Shaker Gifts follow her through life.*

Contents

Preface   9

Seeking Paradise: 13
  Thomas Merton and the Shakers
  by Paul M. Pearson

Pleasant Hill: 54
  A Shaker Village in Kentucky

Introduction to *Religion in Wood:*   72
  A Book of Shaker Furniture

Work and the Shakers: 90
  A Transcript of a Conference Given by
  Thomas Merton at the Abbey of Gethsemani
  on July 22, 1964

Selected Correspondence   106

Bibliography   124

PREFACE This book is a celebration of Merton's love of the Shakers. The Shakers and the Shaker Village of Pleasant Hill in Kentucky are frequently mentioned by Merton in his journals for the last ten years of his life, and over the years, various aspects of his interest in the Shakers have come to light—essays he wrote about them, a talk he gave to his novices, correspondence with others interested in them, and the photographs he took at Pleasant Hill over the course of a number of visits. Until now, these references have remained scattered which made it impossible to get a complete picture of Merton's interest and understanding of this uniquely American movement.

This book brings together for the first time many of these scattered pieces to provide an overall picture of Merton's interest in the Shakers. Merton's article on Pleasant Hill, first published in *Jubilee,* was republished with some minor changes and corrections in his 1967 collection of essays, *Mystics and Zen Masters.* This article gives us a picture of Merton's general interest in the Shakers, but more specifically in the Shaker Village at Pleasant Hill, to which he was a frequent visitor at this time. Pleasant Hill was also a subject of his growing interest in photography, and many of his images of Pleasant Hill from this period are included.

The introduction Merton wrote in 1964 for Edward Deming Andrews's book *Religion in Wood: A Book of Shaker*

Furniture contains his now-classic comment about Shaker craftsmanship: "The peculiar grace of a Shaker chair is due to the fact that it was made by someone capable of believing that an angel might come and sit on it."[1] This essay, more esoteric than his essay on Pleasant Hill, brings together his interest in the poet William Blake and highlights some of the aspects of the Shaker life and work that so attracted Merton. In this essay Merton also suggests the relevance of the Shakers' charism to contemporary America in the light of his thought on Blake.

The penultimate piece in this volume is a transcript of a tape recording of a conference Merton gave to the novices at Gethsemani in July 1964. The conference focuses on the theme of work, a topic of importance to both the Shakers and to monks following the Rule of St. Benedict. The conference has been edited minimally so as to keep as closely as possible to Merton's spoken word while omitting certain repeated words and phrases which were characteristic of Merton's lecturing style but which distract from his overall message. This talk on work conveys one of the essential qualities that attracted Merton to the Shakers.

Thomas Merton's joy and enthusiasm for the Shakers is clearly evident in his correspondence with Edward Deming Andrews. The eminent Shaker authority and the always enthusiastic monk unite in their common interest in a true union of spirits. This key correspondence is augmented by a number of

---

[1] Edward Deming Andrews and Faith Andrews, *Religion in Wood: A Book of Shaker Furniture* (Bloomington: Indiana University Press, 1973), xii.

other, much briefer, groups of letters, many of which sprang from Thomas Merton's contact with Edward Deming Andrews.

Also included is correspondence from Merton to Ralph McCallister and Mary Childs Black. Ralph McCallister in 1962 was the executive director of the nonprofit, educational organization that had been formed the previous year to acquire and restore Pleasant Hill, the closest Shaker Village to the Abbey of Gethsemani. In November 1961 he arranged for Edward Deming Andrews and Faith Andrews to visit Pleasant Hill for a conference and subsequently took them to Gethsemani to meet with Thomas Merton.

Mary Childs Black was director of the Abby Aldrich Rockefeller Folk Art Collection in Williamsburg, Virginia, and was at the time of her correspondence with Merton arranging an exhibit of Shaker spirit drawings which included some pieces from the Andrews' collection.

I would like to thank all those who have contributed to the birth of this book. William H. Shannon and Bernard van Waes for their enthusiasm for the Shakers at the first general meeting of the International Thomas Merton Society in 1989 which inspired my own interest. The first advanced Merton Elderhostel at Bellarmine University in 2002 which forced me into action, inspiring me to put pen to paper and to bring this material together. The Trustees of the Merton Legacy Trust for their support for this project and Robert Ellsberg of Orbis Books for his unfailing enthusiasm from the very beginning. My wife, Helen, for her belief in this book, her proof reading, her suggestions, and her love.

SEEKING PARADISE

Thomas Merton and the Shakers

by Paul M. Pearson

INTRODUCTION   From Thomas Merton's first visit to Pleasant Hill in 1959, up until his last recorded visit there with Canon A. M. (Donald) Allchin in April 1968, he was deeply attracted to this unique American religious sect. After his first visit he wrote in his journal on June 7, 1959:

> *I cannot help seeing Shakertown in a very special light, that of my own vocation. There is a lot of Shakertown in Gethsemani. The two contemporary communities had much in common, were born of the same Spirit. If Shakertown had survived it would probably have evolved much as we have evolved. The prim ladies in their bonnets would have been driving tractors, and the sour gents would have advertised their bread and cheese. And all would have struggled mightily with guilt.*[1]

A very different view from that of Charles Dickens, who wrote of the Shakers over 120 years before Merton's visit on his first American tour:

> *We walked into a grim room where several grim hats were hanging on grim pegs, and the time was grimly told by a grim clock, which uttered every tick with a kind of struggle, as if it broke this grim silence reluctantly and under protest. Ranged against the wall were six or eight stiff high-backed chairs, and they partook so strongly of the general grimness, that one would much rather have sat on the floor than incurred the smallest obligation to any of them.*

---

[1]Thomas Merton, *A Search for Solitude: Pursuing the Monk's True Life*, ed. Lawrence S. Cunningham (San Francisco: HarperCollins, 1996), 287.

Presently, there stalked into this apartment, a grim old Shaker, with eyes as hard, and dull, and cold, as the great round metal buttons on his coat and waistcoat; a sort of calm goblin . . . [2]

THOMAS MERTON'S
INTEREST IN THE
SHAKERS AND
PLEASANT HILL

Merton's earliest reference to the Shakers can be found in his history of the Cistercian Order, *The Waters of Siloe*, where he gives a very brief outline of who the Shakers were. After having noted that they arrived in Kentucky in the same year as the first Trappists, Merton writes:

The Shakers had been brought to America by a certain Ann Lee, a former Quaker, expelled by the Friends because she had some strange ideas. One of her beliefs was that there had to be masculine and feminine principles in the Deity. Word later got round among the Shakers that "Mother Ann" herself was the feminine principle. In spite of their peculiar theology, the Shakers were much safer people to have for neighbours than the Philistines. They were quiet, sober, hard-working men and women who segregated themselves into communistic villages of their own where they lived in celibacy, practiced their religion, and supported themselves by farming and various crafts. In spite of the note of derision in the nickname they received, the Shakers did not go in for violent ceremonies. They did a little sober dancing and handclapping—the men and women dancing as they lived, in separate groups. Eventually the Kentucky

---

[2]Charles Dickens, *American Notes for General Circulation* (Harmondsworth, UK: Penguin, 1972), 257.

Shakers, who took celibacy seriously, all died out. The plain, solid brick buildings of their old village now remain as a curiosity for sightseers.[3]

Merton makes no further reference to the Shakers until his first visit to Pleasant Hill in June 1959. From then, up until his death in 1968, Merton records a number of visits to Pleasant Hill, at least six. Besides these visits, Merton writes of the Shakers in two published essays: "Pleasant Hill: A Shaker Village in Kentucky," first published in the magazine *Jubilee* and later reprinted in the volume *Mystics and Zen Masters,* and an introduction he wrote for Edward Deming Andrews's book *Religion in Wood.* Between 1960 and 1964 Merton corresponded with Edward Deming Andrews, and then after Andrews's death in 1964, for a short time he corresponded with his widow, Faith Andrews. References to the Shakers also come up in a number of others pieces of Merton's correspondence with Mary Childs Black, Ralph McCallister, Robert Meader (director of the Shaker Museum at Old Chatham), Br. Thomas Whitaker of St. Maur's Priory at South Union, and Sr. Prisca and Mother Benedict of the Regina Laudis Community, as well as brief correspondence with a Shaker eldress at the Shaker community of Canterbury.

Merton's interest in the Shakers, I believe, his sense of affinity with them, is based on two foundations. Firstly, his

---

[3]Thomas Merton, *The Waters of Siloe* (New York: Harcourt Brace and Company, 1949), 67.

wholehearted and unfailing embrace of monasticism—
though not necessarily monasticism as it was being practiced
in the forties, fifties, and sixties, but the ideal of monasticism
as he saw it in the desert fathers, St. Benedict, and in the
founding fathers of the Cistercian Order—rather than in its
later reforms. Then secondly, but related to this, Merton's
vision of paradise in the world, his sense of what has been
called "paradise consciousness," original blessing, a sense
which is so evident in his later poetry but can also be seen in
his early interest in the Franciscans, then in the Celtic monks
and in writers such as William Blake, Rainer Maria Rilke,
and Louis Zukofsky. Related to these two foundations there
is also what Michael Higgins calls Merton's Blakean rebellion[4]—his readiness to stand up against the culture of his day
as a prophetic witness to truths different from those held by
the majority and endlessly bombarded at us through adver-
tising and media.

Merton's first visits to Pleasant Hill were in 1959, first in
June and again on December 22. One senses in his early visits that he knows a little of their background, but was not yet
doing much serious reading about them. In June he speaks of
"the big old dormitories" standing "among the weeds in des-
olation," yet sensing there was still "something young about
the old buildings, as if their pioneer hopefulness were still in
them, as if they could not despair though the Shakers were

---

[4]Michael Higgins, "Monasticism as Rebellion: The Blakean Roots of
Merton's Thought," *American Benedictine Review* 39:2 (June 1988):
178-87.

all gone."[5] When he visited Pleasant Hill next in December he got to go inside some of the buildings for the first time and describes the Trustees Office, famous for its winding double staircase, one staircase for the men and one for the women. Merton writes of the

marvelous double winding stair going up to the mysterious clarity of a dome on the roof . . . quiet sunlight filtering in—a big Lebanon cedar outside one of the windows ... All the other houses are locked up. There is Shaker furniture only in the center family house. I tried to get in it and a gloomy old man living in the back told me curtly "it was locked up." The empty fields, the big trees—how I would love to explore those houses and listen to that silence. In spite of the general decay and despair there is joy there still and simplicity.[6]

He concludes saying, "Shakers fascinate me . . . I want to study them."

Early in March 1960 Merton records receiving a letter from a Shaker eldress in reply to an inquiry he sent her. He writes of the Shakers as being

something of a sign—mystery—a strange misguided attempt at utter honesty that wanted to be too pure—but ended up by being nevertheless pure and good, though in many ways absurd. This loyalty, absolute loyalty to a vision leading nowhere. But do such visions really lead nowhere? What they did they did, and it was

---

[5]Merton, *Search for Solitude*, 286.
[6]Ibid., 362.

impressive. It haunts me, at times. I mean the atmosphere and spirit, the image they created, the archetype.[7]

A few days later he records in his journal that he now has some books on the Shakers, though he doesn't record which, and laments not getting around to reading and studying them.[8]

Prior to Merton's next entry in his journals, he started his

---

[7]Ibid., 378.
[8]Ibid., 379.

correspondence with Edward Deming Andrews, the renowned Shaker scholar. The correspondence was initiated by Andrews in late November 1960. Andrews heard of Merton's interest in writing a book on the Shakers to be illustrated by photographs taken by Shirley Burden, and he wrote to offer any assistance he could to the project. Merton had worked with Burden on the book *God Is My Life: The Story of Our Lady of Gethsemani*, which was published in 1960, and although the project to work on a book about the Shakers together was discussed in Merton's correspondence with Burden, nothing ever came of it.

In responding to the letter from Edward Deming Andrews, Merton mentions he has seen a number of his books including *The People Called Shakers* and *Shaker Furniture*. He then goes on briefly to describe his plans for a book about the Shakers:

My part would not be precisely a study of their religion, if by that is to be understood their doctrines, but of their spirit and I might say their mysticism, in practice, as evidenced by their life and their craftsmanship. To me the Shakers are of very great significance, besides being something of a mystery, by their wonderful integration of the spiritual and the physical in their work. There is no question in my mind that one of the finest and most genuine religious expressions of the nineteenth century is in the silent eloquence of Shaker craftsmanship. I am deeply interested in the thought that a hundred years ago our two communities were so close together, so similar, somehow, in ideals, and yet evidently had no contact with one another.

Merton adds:

I will not rush at it and I will try to profit by their example and put into practice some of their careful and honest principles. It would be a crime to treat them superficially, and without the deepest love, reverence and understanding. There can be so much meaning to a study of this kind: meaning for twentieth century America which has lost so much in the last hundred years—lost while seeming to gain. I think the extinction of the Shakers and of their particular kind of spirit is an awful portent. I feel all the more akin to them because our own Order, the Cistercians, originally had the same kind of ideal of honesty, simplicity, good work, for a spiritual motive.[9]

In November 1961 Merton met Edward Deming and Faith Andrews for the first and only time. They were in Kentucky at the invitation of Ralph McCallister, who was at that time executive director of the organization working to restore Pleasant Hill. They visited Merton at Gethsemani, along with McCallister, and Merton had the opportunity to discuss the plans for the restoration of Pleasant Hill. In a memoir, published posthumously, Andrews recalled his visit to Gethsemani:

The visit to the Trappist monastery was a memorable one. At Father Merton's suggestion we arrived in time to attend the short choral office of Nones which was chanted at 1:15 in the afternoon. We met the good brother in a room reserved for visitors,

---

[9]Thomas Merton to Edward Deming Andrews, December 12, 1960.

and then he took me on a tour of the Abbey. (The rules forbade Faith from accompanying us.) Though the monastic rule of silence prevailed, in his role as guide and director of novices he was permitted to speak, answering all questions most graciously and with deep insight into the dedicated work of the order. In the book store we selected a volume we wanted to buy—God Is My Life, with photographs of Gethsemani by Shirley Burden and a foreword by Thomas Merton—but he insisted on presenting it to us. "You can buy books elsewhere," he said, "but not here." Nor would he take money for the famed Trappist cheese, so Faith put the money in the poor box. After an hour or so of the best of good talk, we took our leave, gently waved away by one whom we had already come to regard as a spiritual mentor and intimate friend.[10]

Merton next visited Pleasant Hill on January 12, 1962. On a journey to and back from Asbury Methodist Seminary in Wilmore, he stopped to take pictures and wrote in his journal:

Marvelous, silent, vast spaces around the old buildings. Cold, pure light, and some grand trees. So cold my finger could no longer feel the shutter release. Some marvelous subjects. How the blank side of a frame house can be so completely beautiful I cannot imagine. A completely miraculous achievement of forms.

The moments of eloquent silence and emptiness in Shakertown stayed with me more than anything else—like a vision.[11]

---

[10]Edward Deming Andrews and Faith Andrews, *Fruits of the Shaker Tree of Life: Memoirs of Fifty Years of Collecting and Research* (Stockbridge, MA: Berkshire Traveller Press, 1975), 172.

[11]Thomas Merton, *Turning toward the World: The Pivotal Years*, ed. Victor A. Kramer (San Francisco: HarperCollins, 1996), 194.

One can see the continued influence of the Shakers and Pleasant Hill on Merton over an extensive period of time, culminating in the first of his two published essays on them. In 1963 he records that on October 22 he wrote what he described as "a little article on the Shakers at Pleasant Hill"[12] which he was thinking of publishing in the journal *Jubilee*, founded and edited by his Columbia friend Ed Rice. The *Jubilee* article, illustrated with two of Merton's own photographs of Pleasant Hill, was published in the January 1964 issue of *Jubilee* with the wonderful title "The Shakers: American Celibates and Craftsmen Who Danced in the

---

[12]Thomas Merton, *Dancing in the Water of Life: Seeking Peace at the Hermitage,* ed. Robert E. Daggy (San Francisco: HarperCollins, 1997), 26.

Glory of God."[13] Merton notes in his journal the following month that "I have more (good) reactions to the article on the Shakers . . . than to almost any such thing I have written."[14]

Edward Deming Andrews was among those who wrote in response to his article in *Jubilee,* and in the same letter Andrews asked Merton to write a brief introduction to a new book he was writing on Shaker furniture. In requesting Merton to write this introduction Andrews said of Merton, "I know of no one who has caught so truthfully the spirit which animated the Shaker craftsmen."[15] Merton accepted Andrews's invitation, although he notes he has been refusing such invitations lately; however, "I love the Shakers and all that they have left us far too much to be able to say no."[16] Edward Deming Andrews sent Merton a copy of the manuscript of *Religion in Wood* on March 24, 1964, so that Merton could read the text prior to writing his introduction.

Merton did not get around to writing his introduction to *Religion in Wood* until July 1964, by which time Edward Deming Andrews had died.[17] After the rumor of Edward Deming Andrews's death was confirmed for Merton in the monastery, he wrote to Faith Andrews in late July offering words of consolation to her and praise for her husband's work:

---

[13]Thomas Merton, "The Shakers: American Celibates and Craftsmen Who Danced in the Glory of God," *Jubilee* 11 (January 1964): 36-41.

[14]Merton, *Dancing in the Water of Life,* 72.

[15]Edward Deming Andrews to Thomas Merton, January 21, 1964.

[16]Thomas Merton to Edward Deming Andrews, January 29, 1964.

[17]Edward Deming Andrews died on June 13, 1964.

His vocation was to keep alive the Shaker spirit in its purity and mediate that to the rest of us. I feel personally very much in debt to him for this. I realize more and more the vital importance of the Shaker "gift of simplicity" which is a true American charism: alas, not as fully appreciated as it should be. Ted was faithful to his call, and his work has borne more fruit than we can estimate on this earth. His reward will surely be with those angelic ones whose work and life he understood and shared.[18]

Merton also assured her that after some delays the preface to *Religion in Wood* was finished and was being retyped. After receiving the preface Faith wrote to Merton saying how beautiful she found it, adding she had read it every day since it arrived, "almost a month ago."[19] Merton corresponded with Faith Andrews a few times in the subsequent months with the last extant piece of correspondence dating from April 1965 in which Merton asked about progress in her plans to publish *Religion in Wood*. The book was eventually published in 1966 by Indiana University Press.

In May 1965 Merton visited Pleasant Hill once again, this time with his friend and publisher James Laughlin.[20] In June 1965 he passed through Pleasant Hill while returning from a visit to Lexington, mentioning briefly in his personal journal "new aspects of the wonderful Shaker houses" which he had seen, noting their "inexhaustible variety and dignity in

---

[18]Thomas Merton to Faith Andrews, July 20, 1964.

[19]Faith Andrews to Thomas Merton, August 18, 1964.

[20]Thomas Merton, *A Vow of Conversation* (Basingstoke, Hants., UK: Lamp Press, 1988), 181.

sameness."[21] Merton developed this journal entry considerably in preparing it for publication in *A Vow of Conversation* writing:

The old Shaker colony at Pleasant Hill is a place that always impresses me with awe and creates in me a sense of quiet joy. I love those old buildings and I love the way the road swings up to them. They stand there in an inexpressible dignity, simplicity, and peace under the big trees. They are completely empty now. There have been no more Shakers there for a long time.[22]

Merton's final visit to Pleasant Hill was in April 1968. The visit, made with Canon A. M. (Donald) Allchin and a seminarian from General Theological Seminary in New York was, as Merton records, in the "pelting rain,"[23] and they quickly moved on to visit Ralph Eugene Meatyard and Carolyn Hammer in Lexington. Later that day, while still out with Donald Allchin, they heard the news that Martin Luther King, Jr., had been assassinated in Memphis.

MONKS AND
SHAKERS

Merton was deeply committed to the monastic life, and many years before Vatican II called upon religious orders to go back to their sources, Merton was translating and pursuing studies in the Fathers of the Church, the Desert Fathers, and the various manifestations of monasti-

---

[21] Merton, *Dancing in the Water of Life*, 254.

[22] Merton, *Vow of Conversation*, 187-88.

[23] Thomas Merton, *The Other Side of the Mountain: The End of the Journey*, ed. Patrick Hart (San Francisco: HarperCollins, 1998), 77.

cism that eventually led to St. Benedict's development of his rule for monasteries in the fifth century, and then later to the development of his own Cistercian Order. Alongside this Merton was interested in the flowering of the monastic life in other Christian denominations and, beyond that, in other faiths. The Shakers, as they developed, were essentially monastic—communities of men and women living celibate lives, around a structured life of work and prayer.

In the Christian church the movement from which monasticism developed began during the time of the Emperor Constantine when Christianity became the established religion of the Roman Empire. Men and women fled to the desert regions of Egypt and Syria looking for a more austere and rigorous religious life than that offered by the recently established Christian church. Similarly, the Shakers sought to establish a completely new society separate from what they saw as the corruption of their time. They went to an area of relative wilderness and set about attempting to cultivate it in peace and to build the Kingdom of God on earth.

The Shakers did not take vows as such, but the covenant that they signed on fully adopting the Shaker way of life involved a commitment to celibacy, confession and community of goods—three "C's" for which they were frequently criticized as being Papists. The model they used for their development was the early Christian church where "all who believed were together and had all things in common; and they sold their possessions and goods and distributed them to all, as they

had need"[24]—a model of community that has only really been achieved in some manifestations of the monastic life.

The Cistercians took three vows, in line with the Rule of St. Benedict—obedience, stability, and *conversatio morum*—

---

[24]Acts 2:44-45.

conversion of manners, or conversion of life, a vow which incorporated celibacy and poverty. In the Rule of St. Benedict obedience and *conversatio morum* included manifesting one's conscience to one's superior, similar to the confession practiced by the Shakers. Similarly, the Shakers were obedient to the elders of the community and the ministry and, though not taking a vow of stability, chose freely to stay in the initial Shaker family which they joined. For both Shakers and monks their respective "Millennial Laws" and the Rule of St. Benedict governed not just the spiritual life of the community but its temporal life as well—the day's work, clothing, sleeping arrangements, and how children and infirm and aged members of the community were to be treated.

There are numerous other parallels between the Shakers and monastic life following the Rule of St. Benedict—new members aspiring to join either community followed a special novitiate regime until they were judged to be ready for full admission to the community. The Rule of St. Benedict instructed the monk to welcome all strangers as Christ, a precept followed closely by the Shakers. The Rule emphasized the importance of continually seeking God, again a precept witnessed to by the Shakers, in the words of Mother Ann: "labor to make the way of God your own; let it be your inheritance, your treasure, your occupation, your daily calling."[25] In both communities members away on a journey were

---

[25]Thomas Merton, "Introduction" to Edward Deming Andrews and Faith Andrews, *Religion in Wood: A Book of Shaker Furniture* (Bloomington: Indiana University Press, 1973), ix.

instructed to follow the community's life of prayer and, upon their return, not to disturb the life of the community by telling tales of what they had seen on their travels. In neither community could a gift be received without permission from the abbot or elder. Both the abbot and elder were subject to the same rules as the community and shared in its common life. Provision was made in both ways of life for receiving "backsliders" back into the community, and both relegated such backsliders to the lowest place in the community.

Both ways of life stressed the virtue of humility. The chapter of the Rule of St. Benedict on humility is one of the longest and most structured chapters of his rule as he lays out the twelve steps of humility. Similarly, the Shakers were admonished about using superfluous decoration and encouraged to avoid things that were expensive and extravagant. The Shakers' belief in humility is summed up succinctly in many of their songs, including their most famous one, "The Gift to Be Simple":

When true simplicity is gain'd,
To bow and to bend we shan't be ashamed,
To turn, turn will be our delight
'Till by turning, turning we come round right.[26]

Merton writes of the humility practiced by the Shakers saying:

The Shakers remain as witnesses to the fact that only humil-

[26]Edward Deming Andrews, *The Gift to Be Simple: Songs, Dances and Rituals of the American Shakers* (New York: Dover Publications, 1940), 136.

ity keeps man in communion with truth, and first of all with his own inner truth. This one must know without knowing it, as they did. For as soon as a man becomes aware of "his truth" he lets go of it and embraces an illusion.[27]

In the Rule of St. Benedict the craftsmen of the monastery were instructed to practice their crafts "with all humility," and if a monk gets a "swollen head because of his skill in his craft," the Abbot was not to allow him to practice that craft again until "his pride has been humbled."[28] Similarly, a Shaker could be moved from a particular craft if there was evidence of "unseemly pride."[29]

However, beyond these immediate similarities, I think there are a number of particular elements that attracted Merton. Firstly, Merton was struck by the Shakers understanding of work—manual labor was central to the life of the early monks and there still continues a strong tradition among the Cistercians of earning their daily bread by the work of their hands. In Merton's early days at Gethsemani this was frequently work in the fields, though later, due to financial necessity, the manufacturing work of producing cheese, fruitcake, and fudge developed. Within many traditions one can identify the concept that work, manual labor, helps to purify the soul and bring it closer to God. Any chore in either the monastic or Shaker life could become an opportunity to serve

---

[27]Thomas Merton to Edward Deming Andrews, December 21, 1961.

[28]*The Rule of St. Benedict for Monasteries*, trans. Dom Bernard Basil Bolton (n.p., 1969), chap. 57.

[29]Andrews and Andrews, *Religion in Wood*, 10.

both God and the community. Within the Buddhist tradition this is called "mindfulness"; in business circles managers would call it "focus"; for the Shakers it is summed up in their motto "put your hands to work and your hearts to God,"[30] or again in another saying, "a man can show his religion as much in measuring onions as he can in singing hallelujah."[31]

Merton was a strong advocate of manual labor in the monastic life, but he best witnesses to the holiness of work in his descriptions of the regular round of chores in his life at the hermitage. His essay "Day of a Stranger" clearly describes the rhythm of his hermit life, the daily chores of the hermitage all embraced with mindfulness and given as much importance as his prayer and his work of writing. In a letter of this time Merton writes of his work:

Cutting wood, clearing ground, cutting grass, cooking soup, drinking fruit juice, sweating, washing, making fire, smelling smoke, sweeping, etc. This is religion. The further one gets away from this, the more one sinks in the mud of words and gestures. The flies gather.[32]

Merton is here emphasizing, as St. Benedict does in his rule, the sacredness of work. St. Benedict compares the workman's tools to the chalice and other tools of the altar,

[30]Suzanne Skees, *God among the Shakers: A Search for Stillness and Faith at Sabbathday Lake* (New York: Hyperion, 1998), 168.

[31]Ibid., 176.

[32]Thomas Merton, *The Courage for Truth: The Letters of Thomas Merton to Writers*, selected and edited by Christine M. Bochen (New York: Farrar, Straus and Giroux, 1993), 225.

instructing the cellarer of the monastery that "the monastery utensils and all its belongings he is to regard as if they were the sacred vessels of the altar."[33] Similarly, for the Shakers, work equaled prayer and one could achieve a meditative state of worship in whatever task one was doing because all work was undertaken for God. Their religious rituals "valorized" all work, especially "women's work," which was thus elevated to the same status as men's work—both were essential to the survival of the community.

This idea of work as worship did not mean the work was poorly done as the monks or the Shakers focused their minds on other, less worldly things. Doing the work well was worship, and so the Shakers excelled as craftsmen and their name became associated with quality products—seeds, furniture, brooms, clothing, boxes. Merton also expressed this attraction to quality. Tasks that he undertook around the monastery he attempted to do to the best of his ability. For example, when he was appointed forester, he set about learning all that he could about the Gethsemani woods, about the different trees, their life cycles, and issues of concern arising about the lack of reforestation. It can also be seen in his desire to have some of his works published by fine letter presses where great care was taken in creating fine-quality editions of his work—the books printed by Victor Hammer and by Stanbrook Abbey are good examples of this desire. In addition, there is also Merton's artistic temperament. The son of artists and a friend of poets and artists, Merton also had artis-

---

[33] *Rule of St. Benedict*, chap. 31.

tic talents displayed in his prose and poetry, his drawings and calligraphies, and his photographs. In writing of his father, Owen, in *The Seven Storey Mountain*, Merton points to some typically Cistercian or Shaker trends in his father's art work:

His vision of the world was sane, full of balance, full of veneration for structure, for the relations of masses and for the circumstances that impress an individual identity on each created thing. His vision was religious and clean, and therefore his paintings were without decoration or superfluous comment, since a religious man respects the power of God's creation to bear witness for itself.[34]

A second factor that attracted Merton to the Shakers was, I would suggest, their stress on simplicity and their understanding of their relationship to the place where they lived and the natural world they shared with that place. During the 1940s Merton was working on a history of the Cistercian Order and its American foundations, published in 1949 as *The Waters of Siloe*. Merton's early descriptions of the order in this book are very Franciscan in their simplicity and appreciation of nature and a far cry from the seventeenth-century reforms of the order or the strict observance followed at Gethsemani under Dom Fredrick Dunne at the time Merton was writing this book. Merton's descriptions of the early Cistercians mirror his own growing experience of place and nature. For example, he writes in *The Waters of Siloe:*

[34]Thomas Merton, *The Seven Storey Mountain* (London: Sheldon Press, 1975), 3.

Forest and field, sun and wind and sky, earth and water, all speak the same silent language, reminding the monk that he is here to develop like the things that grow all around him . . . even the site of a Cistercian monastery is, or ought to be, a lesson in contemplation.[35]

He also writes:

When the monks had found their homes, they not only settled there, for better or for worse, but they sank their roots into the ground and fell in love with their woods. Indeed, this love of one's monastery and its surroundings is something integral to the Cistercian life. It forms the object of a special vow: stability.[36]

Merton also points to the way the early Cistercian monasteries developed within the order "a beautiful spiritual symbolism by their names alone—eloquent and harmonious names full of poetry and simple mysticism." Through being "steeped in the language and imagery of Scripture, the Cistercians were acutely alive to the spiritual and poetic possibilities of their surroundings, which they condensed into names like Fountains, Clairvaux ('Clear Valley,' or 'Valley of Light'), Trois Fontaines ('Three Fountains'), Vauluisant ('Shining Valley') . . . Mellifont ('Fount of Honey')."[37] The Shakers, like the early Cistercians, appreciated the importance of place. They carefully chose sites for their communities, and often the place and their religious aspirations were reflected in

---

[35]Merton, *Waters of Siloe*, 274.
[36]Ibid., 273.
[37]Ibid.

the names they gave their communities—Pleasant Hill, New Lebanon, and Sabbathday Lake, for example.

This sense of place in both the Shakers and the Cistercians embraced the architecture of their buildings, an architecture characterized by its simplicity. At times, through various influences, both communities have lost this spirit. It has been rediscovered within the Cistercian Order in the reforms occurring as a result of the liturgical movement of the last century and the Second Vatican Council. However, before these changes, Merton touched on the qualities of Cistercian architecture in *The Waters of Siloe:*

> *Cistercian architecture is famous for its energy and simplicity and purity, for its originality and technical brilliance. It was the Cistercians who effected the transition from the massive, ponderous Norman style to the thirteenth-century Gothic, with its genius for poising masses of stone in mid-air, and making masonry fly and hover over the low earth with the self-assurance of an angel.*[38]

> *The typical Cistercian church, with its low elevation, its plain, bare walls, lighted by few windows and without stained glass, achieved its effect by the balance of masses and austere, powerful, round or pointed arches and mighty vaulting. These buildings filled anyone who entered them with peace and restfulness and disposed the soul for contemplation in an atmosphere of simplicity and poverty.*[39]

---

[38]Ibid., 14.
[39]Ibid.

These descriptions could be applied equally well to a great deal of Shaker architecture. Merton's words in those quotations remind me specifically of the great round stone barn at the Shaker Village of Hancock in Massachusetts. This barn, built in 1826, has the feel of a cathedral. While there visiting the village I was struck with wonder upon entering the barn, a sense of awe at the harmonious effect of light, scent, architecture, and wood, experienced as a deep sense of peace. The building, as Merton said, "hovered over the low earth with the self-assurance of an angel." Yet its beauty does not detract from the highly practical and technically brilliant architecture of the building. Merton saw a photograph taken by Shirley Burden of a stone Shaker barn near Harvard which he says was "very Cistercian indeed," commenting "there are many interesting statutes of the General Chapters concerning architecture, decoration etc."[40]

Writing many years later about the Shakers, after having visited Pleasant Hill, Merton commented on the "extraordinary, unforgettable beauty" of their buildings and furniture brought about, like the Cistercians, through their attempts to "build honest buildings and to make honest sturdy pieces of furniture."[41] Merton also refers to this in some of his unpublished notes describing examples of work sensitive to *logoi*, to the true Word spoken by God:

> *Shaker handicrafts, and furniture. Deeply impregnated by the communal mystique of the Shaker community. The simplicity and austerity demanded by their way of life enabled an unconscious spiritual purity to manifest itself in full clarity. Shaker handicrafts are then a real* epiphany of logoi.
>
> *Characterized by* spiritual *light.*
>
> *See also their buildings. Barns especially. Highly mystical quality: Capaciousness, dignity, solidity, permanence.* Logos *of a barn? "But my wheat, gather ye into my barn."*
>
> *Note: It is never a question of a "barn" in the abstract and in no definite place: the Shaker farm building always fits right*

---

[40]Thomas Merton to Edward Deming Andrews, January 17, 1961.

[41]Thomas Merton, *Mystics and Zen Masters* (New York: The Noonday Press, 1988), 198.

into its location, manifests the logos *of the place where it is built, grasps and expresses the hidden* logos *of the valley, or hillside, etc. which forms its site.* Logos of the site. *Important in Cistercian monasteries of twelfth century.*[42]

Merton picks up this same theme in relation to Shaker furniture in his introduction to *Religion in Wood*, writing that "neither the Shakers nor Blake would be disturbed at the thought that a work-a-day bench, cupboard, or table might also and at the same time be furniture in and for heaven."[43] This description can be applied equally well to Shaker and Cistercian architecture. Shaker architecture creates, in the words of Andrews, "an atmosphere of settledness and repose" which pervaded the Shaker villages "as though they were part of the land itself"[44]—a reflection equally applicable to Cistercian architecture.

PARADISE
CONSCIOUSNESS
—ORIGINAL
BLESSING

Merton's attraction to the simplicity of the Shakers, to their search for what he saw as the core spirit, the *logos* of a thing, mirrors a trend in Merton's own thought and writing, a pursuit of paradise consciousness. This sense of paradise consciousness comes across strongly in some of

[42]Thomas Merton, *Ascetical and Mystical Theology: An Introduction to Christian Mysticism (From the Apostolic Fathers to the Council of Trent)*, 64. Mimeographed copy of lectures given at the Abbey of Gethsemani in the archives of the Thomas Merton Center, Bellarmine University, Louisville, Kentucky.

[43]Andrews and Andrews, *Religion in Wood*, viii.

[44]Merton, *Mystics and Zen Masters*, 199.

Merton's later poetry; in his journals, especially as his celebration of the world of nature around him develops; in his photographs, where ordinary objects could portray an extraordinary, unexpected beauty; and in many of the subjects in which he expresses an interest. It is central, for example, to many of the poets and writers Merton was reading—William Blake, Gerard Manley Hopkins, Rainer Maria Rilke, Boris Pasternak, Louis Zukofsky, and Edwin Muir, to name but a few.

Merton spoke to the monastic community at Gethsemani a number of times in 1965 and 1966 about Rilke's poetry, and in one talk he spoke of Rilke's poetic view of reality—inseeing—in terms reminiscent of some of his comments on the Shakers. Merton described Rilke's inseeing as a deep encounter between the poet and his subject, getting right into the center of the subject, right into the heart. In one conference Merton describes the way Rilke gets into the very center of the thing he is describing. Taking a dog as an example, this inseeing involves getting into

the dog's very center, the point from where it begins to be a dog, the place in which, in it, where God, as it were, would have sat down for a moment when the dog was finished in order to watch it under the influence of its first embarrassments and inspirations and to know that it was good, that nothing was lacking, that it could not have been made better.[45]

---

[45]Thomas Merton, *Natural Contemplation* (Kansas City: Credence Cassettes, 1987), transcribed by the current author.

It was this same spirit that Merton was attracted to in the Shakers. Their architecture and their furniture were made, so they believed, as God would have made it; it could not have been made better.

The essential Shaker message was deeply Christian. Unlike many Puritan sects they were not "men of a dour, sulphur-and-brimstone eschatology" but, as Merton writes, "simple, joyous, optimistic people whose joy was rooted in the fact that Christ *had* come, and that the basic Christian experience was the discovery of Christ living in us all now" believing in "a redeemed cosmos in which war, hatred, tyranny, and greed had no place—a cosmos of creativity and worship."[46] In Shaker work there is a certain Edenic innocence as each item that the craftsman makes is a participation in God's work of creation and the craftsman's ideal was to make each object to best fulfill its vocation. This gave their work "an inimitable honesty," as Merton famously says, "the peculiar grace of a Shaker chair is due to the fact that it was made by someone capable of believing that an angel might come and sit on it."[47] In both their work and their worship the Shakers attempted to be "attuned to the music intoned in each being by God the Creator and by the Lord Jesus."[48]

---

[46]Merton, "Introduction" to Andrews and Andrews, *Religion in Wood*, ix.
[47]Ibid., xii.
[48]Ibid., ix.

COUNTERCULTURAL
—"ART
DEGRADED,
IMAGINATION
DENIED, WAR
GOVERNED THE
NATIONS."[49]

In the Shakers Merton also found many of the countercultural beliefs that he himself was explicating long before they became popular subjects in the Catholic church—most noticeably their pacifism and their belief in equal rights for all people. The Shakers, like the Quakers from whom they emerged, were pacifists and refused to participate in the American Revolutionary War and did not take sides in the American Civil War. They felt that war and violence were related to sex and marriage, believing that "those who marry will fight"[50] and that lust and cruelty went together. Merton also came from a pacifist background: his mother, Ruth, was a nominal Quaker, and his parents left France soon after Merton's birth to avoid his father, Owen, being called up to fight in the First World War. His concerns about war and violence occur in his writings over the years but are most prominent in his writings of the sixties when, for a time, he was prevented by the Cistercian Order from publishing on the subjects of war and peace and the nuclear arms race.

The Shakers were also great advocates of equal rights. Within their communities there was no distinction between male and female, black and white—all people were viewed and treated as equal. Similarly, Merton was acutely aware of issues relating to racism and discrimination in its various forms. Both Merton and the Shakers criticized the established churches for practicing social injustices and inequalities. In words that Merton felt echoed St. Bernard, one

---

[49]Ibid., xiv. Merton is here quoting from William Blake.
[50]Merton, *Mystics and Zen Masters*, 194

Shaker elder said "the divine man has no right to waste money upon what you would call beauty in his house or daily life, while there are people living in misery."[51]

There is at times in Merton an almost Luddite attitude to technology and technological progress. Although the Shakers were great inventors and were happy to embrace the latest technology, their motives for doing so remained pure, and this must have been attractive for Merton. Merton writes of their work's inimitable honesty which "one cannot find in the slick new model of the latest car, tailored like some unearthly reptilian fowl and flashing with pointless gadgetry, marketed to replace other models designed for obsolescence, and to be replaced itself without delay."[52] He asks whether it is still possible in our own time for the Shaker spirit to exist when our "lives are in full technological, sociological, and spiritual upheaval"—can Shaker craftsmanship and its spirit "find a way to direct and inform machine production?"[53] These are questions as valid today as they were when Merton posed them.

For Merton, the Shakers "exemplified the simplicity, the practicality, the earnestness, and the hope that have been associated with the United States," and they acted out their conviction with a full awareness of the world around them, aware that the serpent had already entered into the paradise of the New World, that

---

[51]Ibid., 197.

[52]Merton, "Introduction" to Andrews and Andrews, *Religion in Wood*, x.

[53]Ibid., xv.

already the irresponsible waste of mine and forest, of water and land, the destruction of bison and elk, were there to show that Paradise was not indefinitely self-sustaining.[54]

They were also aware, as Merton wrote of the Shakers in a Cold War Letter[55] to Mary Childs Black, that

---

[54]Ibid., xii-xiii.

[55]At the height of the Cold War, when Merton was forbidden to publish on issues relating to war and peace, he privately circulated a collection of over one hundred of his letters that related to these issues. He called this collection "The Cold War Letters."

*it was a paradise in which the Indian had been slaughtered and the Negro was enslaved. In which the immigrant was treated as an inferior being, and in which he had to work very hard for the "gold" that was to be "picked up in the streets." *[56]

But against their critique of the world, both Merton and the Shakers found hope through their deep faith in the ulti-

[56]Thomas Merton to Mary Childs Black, January 24, 1962.

mate goodness of humanity and creation, through their search for paradise. Merton looked for this hope in Latin America, in the work of poets and writers, and in experimental forms of the religious and Christian life. He also found it in the Shaker's "Tree of Life." The image of the Paradise Tree, which had come to the Shakers as a spirit gift, suggested to Merton that

this particular symbolic hope needs to be taken seriously precisely in the moment of darkness and deception when, in our atmosphere of crisis, bitterness, and confusion, this hope has turned for so many into angry despair and the sacred tree has been stripped of those bright leaves and golden fruits.[57]

As he had said in a letter to Faith Andrews after the death of her husband, the Shaker "gift of simplicity" was a "true American charism."[58]

THE DANCE OF CREATION

The areas that Merton highlights within the Shakers seem a long way from Charles Dickens's description of Shaker "grimness." The Shaker gift of music and dance is one more expression of their belief in the power of God among his believers, of paradise consciousness, of realized eschatology, of the presence of God's Kingdom. Merton also commented on the Shaker's gift of music and dance, writing of "the pure, entranced, immaculate dancing, shaking the sex out of their

---

[57]Merton, "Introduction" to Andrews and Andrews, *Religion in Wood*, xii.

[58]Thomas Merton to Faith Andrews, July 20, 1964.

hands. And the whirling . . ." He added in a somewhat wistful tone, "God, at least they had the sense to dance."[59]

In Merton's final years his own sense of music and dance became evident once more. He recalls his mother's interest in dancing, times he himself danced in the hermitage,[60] and his love of jazz during his time at Cambridge and New York. From an old record player in his hermitage, the sounds of jazz and contemporary singers like Bob Dylan, Joan Baez, and the Beatles rang out across the Gethsemani woods. Merton also discovered the importance of music and dance in other mystical traditions—the dance of Shiva in Hinduism and the whirling of the Islamic dervishes.

Merton's embrace of the dance of creation was expressed most succinctly by him in "The General Dance," his closing chapter to his revision of *Seeds of Contemplation*, written at the time of his interest in the Shakers. In one of his letters of this time to Edward Deming Andrews, Merton recalls a visit to Pleasant Hill and looking out of the attic of the guest house (now the Trustee's Office) "through the branches of an old cedar at the quiet field in which they used to dance (Holy Sion's Plain)."[61] He then goes on to tell Andrews of his discovery of an old Christmas carol "about the 'dancing' of God with man in the mystery of the Incarnation," saying "I think here there may be an important lead. The carol is an ancient English one. In it, the Lord

[59]Merton, *Search for Solitude*, 362.
[60]Merton, *Dancing in the Water of Life*, 174.
[61]Thomas Merton to Edward Deming Andrews, January 17, 1961.

speaks of His coming at Christmas in the following words: 'Tomorrow is my dancing day . . .'"[62] Each stanza of the carol concludes with an invitation to sing and to dance. The carol tells the story of Christ from his Incarnation, through his time on earth, concluding with Christ's Ascension:

Then up to Heaven did I ascend,
Where now I dwell in sure substance
On the right hand of God that man
May come unto the general dance.

These words echo Merton's invitation at the end of *New Seeds of Contemplation* inviting us all to join in with the general dance of creation:

The Lord plays and diverts Himself in the garden of His creation, and if we could go out of our own obsession with what we think is the meaning of it all, we might be able to hear His call and follow Him in His mysterious, cosmic dance . . . when, like the Japanese poet Basho we hear an old frog land in a quiet pond with a solitary splash—at such times the awakening, the turning inside out of all values, the "newness," the emptiness and the purity of vision that make themselves evident, provide a glimpse of the cosmic dance.

For the world and time are the dance of the Lord in emptiness. The silence of the spheres is the music of a wedding feast . . . no despair of ours can alter the reality of things, or stain the joy of the cosmic dance which is always there. Indeed, we are in

---

[62]Ibid.

the midst of it, and it is in the midst of us, for it beats in our very blood, whether we want it to or not.

Yet the fact remains that we are invited to forget ourselves on purpose, cast our awful solemnity to the winds and join in the general dance.[63]

Merton invites us, as he wrote in a 1964 message to Latin American poets, to "Come, dervishes: here is the water of life. Dance in it."[64]

---

[63]Thomas Merton, *New Seeds of Contemplation* (New York: New Directions, 1961), 296-297.

[64]Thomas Merton, *Raids on the Unspeakable* (New York: New Directions, 1966), 161.

PLEASANT HILL

A Shaker Village in Kentucky

The Shakers,[1] or rather "The United Society of Believers in Christ's Second Appearing," were most active in New England and upper New York State in the first half of the nineteenth century. They have almost completely died out today. At the time of their greatest expansion, they reached westward and established communities in Ohio, Indiana, and Kentucky. The simple, spacious buildings of the Kentucky Shaker colonies still stand: some of those at South Union were for a time occupied by the Benedictine Priory of St. Maur's. Those at Pleasant Hill, popularly known as "Shakertown," near Lexington, are being restored as a public monument.

As their official title suggests, the "Believers in Christ's Second Appearing" were people who had entirely forsaken secular society to set up a religious and prophetic commune, believing in the imminent end of the world. With them, as perhaps with some of the early monks, celibacy was held to be symbolic of the futility of generating any more human beings in a world ready for destruction and for renewal on an angelic plane. The term "Shakers" is due not only to the dancing and ecstatic experiences which marked their common worship, but perhaps especially to their belief that when the Holy Spirit was present He made Himself known by

---

[1] These pages rely heavily on material collected and published by Edward Deming Andrews, especially in his books *Shaker Furniture* and *The People Called Shakers*. The latter (New York: Oxford University Press, 1953) is the best introduction to Shaker history and thought. It is now being reissued in a new edition by the Indiana University Press.

"shaking" the whole community in a kind of prophetic earthquake. The eschatological charity of the order produced an inward power which, they believed, would "shake" the world and prepare it for the millennial renewal.

The extraordinary theology of the Shakers, with its emphasis on the "Second Appearing" of Christ in a Woman, is only fully to be understood when we recognize its spiritual affinity with Gnosticism and Montanism. Yet there is a great independence and originality in the Shaker spirit. The "Woman," the embodiment of divine Wisdom in the last days of the world, and Daughter of the Holy Spirit, was Mother Ann Lee, who came to America from England with eight companions and landed in New York on the sixth of August, 1774. After gathering a small community at Watervliet, New York, in 1776, she laid the definitive foundations of her society at New Lebanon in 1779.

For many reasons, "ordinary" Americans of those revolutionary times found the Shakers disturbing, and subjected them to persecution. In the first place, the Shakers were pacifists. They refused to participate in the Revolutionary War on either side, which meant that they were considered "agents of the British" by patriotic Americans. Their fervent love of celibacy was closely connected with pacifism, for they held that lust and cruelty went together, and that unchastity led to avarice and attachment to worldly goods, which were protected or acquired by force. "Marriage," they declared, "is not a Christian institution, because the community of goods cannot be maintained therein . . . Wars are the

results of lusts for lands and women. *Those who marry will fight."*

The Shakers, being fully determined to do neither of these things, lived in peaceful, cenobitic communes, in which the sexes were kept firmly apart. In each "Family House," the men had their common dwelling on one side, the women on the other, and they used separate stairways to reach their isolated dormitories. In the last analysis, the real significance of their celibacy was their belief that they had been completely regenerated and were living the perfect risen life in

and with Christ. "We have actually risen with Christ and travel with Him to the resurrection [i.e., of all flesh]," said one of the first Elders. But this rebirth to the angelic life could only be achieved by embracing perfect chastity, without which one could not be a genuine Christian. We can detect echoes of Catharism and Montanism, which, like the religion of the Shakers, placed a great emphasis on virginity and prophetic inspiration and attacked institutional religion. Like the Albigenses, the Shakers believed that the conventional organized "churches" had been reduced, by continual compromises, to complicity with the world in its lusts, its greed for money, and its appetite for power.

They felt that this was amply demonstrated by the social injustices and inequalities which were not only tolerated by most Christians but actively encouraged by them. Therefore, they concluded that the Kingdom of God had not yet been established on earth since the professed followers of Christ were obviously not imitating Him. A Shaker of the Harvard Community wrote in 1853:

[Jesus] was no speculator in stocks, trades, or estates. He could not be distinguished by the carriage He rode in or the palace He dwelt in, nor the cloth He wore, by the multitude of His servants, golden ornaments, nor refined literature . . .

Jesus was a simple carpenter, the apostles were working men, Mother Ann and the early Shakers were all simple working-class people. The Shaker communities lived an austere and disciplined life of renunciation and labor and it was their hard work that eventually won them the respect of their neighbors. Yet at the same time they were shrewd and practical in their dealings with the wicked world, and they sent their most businesslike representatives to market to buy and sell, so that even Emerson remarked caustically on their ability to drive a hard bargain.

We cannot safely judge the Shakers by what was said about them, especially in the beginning. They were accused by their enemies of everything from nudism and debauchery to being "the principal enemies of America." They are famous for the dancing which characterized their worship, and this dancing was a source of grave scandal to other Protestants, who felt that such "bodily agitation" was distinctly "Catholic." In fact, though the Shakers themselves believed that the Church of Rome was the Great Whore of Babylon, along with all the other established institutional forms of Christianity, they themselves were considered to be "Papish" because public general confession of past sins was a prerequisite to admission, and after one was in the Society he had to obey the Ministers in perfect simplicity—a "Romish" practice.

In actual fact, their written records, their simple songs, and especially their "concentrated labor" show these believers to have been sincere, honest, modest people, minding their own business, devoted to their faith in the Second Coming of Christ, living already in another world in which they felt themselves close to the angels and to the Lord of angels, along with Mother Ann, who would soon usher them into the New Creation, the definitive Kingdom.

The most eloquent witness to the Shaker spirit is the fruit of their labor. Anyone who knows anything about furniture

realizes that today a mere stool, a coat hanger, a simple box made by the Shakers, is likely to be worth a good sum: and this not because an artificial market for such things has been created, but because of their consummate perfection, their extraordinary unselfconscious beauty and simplicity. There is, in the work of the Shakers, a beauty that is unrivaled because of its genuine spiritual purity—a quality for which there is no adequate explanation, but which can be account-ed for in part by the doctrine of the Shakers themselves and their monastic view of manual work as an essential part of the Christian life.

Like the earliest monastic documents, they spoke of the "work of God" which they were called upon to do: the work of building God's "Millennial Church." (In pre-Benedictine documents, the *opus Dei* is not just the liturgy but the whole life of monastic conversion and transformation in Christ.) "God," said one of the Shaker Elders, "is the great Artist and Master Builder; the Gospel is the means; the Ministration are his Laborers, and instruments under his direction. We must labor in union with them to cast all rubbish out of and from around the building, and to labor to bring everything both outward and inward, more and more into order."

This allegorization of Shaker spirituality in terms of "work" represents, of course, no mere abstract fantasy. The Shakers were meticulous workers, with a passion for order, cleanliness, simplicity, practicality, and economy of means. In their "Millennial Laws" they decreed that "Believers may not, in any case, manufacture for sale any article or articles which are superfluously wrought, and which would tend to feed the pride and vanity of man," and "Buildings, mouldings and cornices which are merely for fancy may not be made by Believers." Not only were mirrors, silver spoons, gold and silver watches, and silver pencils banned from the communes as "superfluous," but also "silver tooth picks, three bladed knives, superfluous whips, gay silk handkerchiefs, checkered handkerchiefs made by the world, superfluous suspenders of any kind, and flowery painted clocks." Speaking of a frivolous and "showy" taste for ornament, an Elder said: "The divine man has no right to waste money upon what you would call beauty in his house or daily life, while there are people living in misery." The words unconsciously echo a famous passage in St. Bernard's *Apologia* for Cistercian austerity against Cluny. Yet the Shakers, like the first Cistercians, while giving no conscious thought to the *beauty* of their work, sought only to build honest buildings and to make honest and sturdy pieces of furniture. In doing so, they produced buildings and furniture of extraordinary, unforgettable beauty. True, this beauty has not always been obvious to everyone. Dickens thought Shaker furniture looked "grim," and the spiritual loveliness of Shaker simplicity is not evident to the eye that has submitted passively to the perversion of form by commerce (for example, the absurdities of American automobile design in the fifties).

The mind of the Shaker was directed not merely to the good of the work, the *bonum operis,* or to the advantage of the worker, the *bonum operantis,* but to something that tran-

scended and included both: a kind of wholeness and order and worship that filled the whole day and the whole life of the working community. "Put your hands to work and your hearts to God," said Mother Ann, and again, "Clean your room well, for good spirits will not live where there is dirt. There is no dirt in heaven." The Shakers worked well because their work was a worship offered to God in the sight of his angels—a Biblical phrase which sets the tone for the life of the monks according to the Benedictine Rule. As a matter of fact, the early Shakers expressed a belief that their furniture designs and other patterns had been given to them by the angels and that they manifested heavenly forms, not belonging to the world of fallen men. In point of fact, as E. D. Andrews shows, the Shaker designs were derived from early American colonial patterns which were purified and perfected by the zeal of the Shakers for "primitive rectitude" and their "religious care."

In this perfect fusion of temporal and eternal values, of spirit and matter, the Shakers were in all truth living according to a kind of inspired eschatology in which ambition, personal gain, and even quick material results were not considered important. Of course, whatever was made was made for use, and consequently the quality of the work was paramount. What was to be used, was made for "the Church," and in order to share the fruits of labor with the poor and the hungry. The workman had to apply himself to his task with all skill and also with the necessary virtues of humility, patience, and love, contributing thereby to the peace and order of the common life, and "supporting the structure of fraternity."

In no case was work to be done in a hurry or under pressure, or indeed under any form of spiritual compulsion. The competitive spirit was banned because of its occult relationship with lust and violence. Overworking was frowned upon. The workers were encouraged to engage in a variety of tasks, to escape obsession and attachment. At all times their work had to be carried on at a steady, peaceful rhythm, for, as one of the Elders said: "We are not called to labor to excel, or to be like the world; but to excel them in order, union, peace and in good works—works that are truly virtuous and useful to man in this life." He also said: "All work done or things made in the Church for their own use ought to be faithfully and well done, but plain and without superfluity. All things ought to be made according to their order and use." Therefore, as E. D. Andrews says, "an atmosphere of settledness and repose pervaded the [Shaker] villages, as though they were part of the land itself."

Shoddy and hasty workmanship was condemned as "worldly" and unworthy of those living the divine life. Once, when someone had a vision to the effect that brass doorknobs were useless and "worldly," a brother spent considerable time removing all the brass knobs and replacing them with wooden ones.

Some of the sayings of Mother Ann, and other "Shaker sermonettes," give us more light on this attitude of mind, which consisted fundamentally in a devotion to *truth*. A thing or a person is perfect insofar as it is what it is meant to be. Absolute flawlessness is impossible, and the Shakers had no unrealistic dreams about utter perfection. But they were very realistic in striving to make things as they ought to be made so that they served their purpose well. They strove in all things for truth, and made a point of simply *being themselves*. "Do be natural," one of these maxims tells us, "a poor diamond is better than an imitation." "Do not be troubled because you have no great virtues. God made a million spears of grass where He made one tree." "Do be truthful; do avoid exaggeration; if you mean a mile, say a mile, and if

you mean one, say one, and not a dozen." "Whatever is really useful is virtuous though it does not at first seem so." Sometimes the simple Shaker maxims remind one of William Blake. This one, for instance: "Order is the creation of beauty. It is heaven's first law, and the protection of souls." Or especially this other: *"Every force evolves a form."*

When we ponder these statements, we discover that they

are full of wisdom. They bear witness to a soundness of judgment and a sanity of vision that help to account for the wonders of Shaker craftsmanship: underlying it all is a quasi-mystical sense of *being* and of *reality* crystallized in this simple maxim, which, for all its technical imprecision, reflects something of the great religious philosophies of all time: *"Sincerity is the property of the universe."*

The Shakers came to Kentucky and established themselves at Pleasant Hill, "the topmost bough upon the tree" and "the cream of Kentucky," in 1806. It was indeed pleasant, rolling farm land, a mile or so from the deep wooded gorge of the Kentucky River. The community consisted of recruits from New York, New Jersey, Pennsylvania, and Virginia. Later members came from Europe, including a large colony of Swedes, who were settled in the West Lot House. In the early days, after surviving the usual persecutions, they built a flourishing little town with workshops rising all around the three main "Families" and the Meeting House. John Dunlavy, one of the first Chief Ministers of Pleasant Hill, is said by E. D. Andrews to have had "a clearer insight into religious communism than any other Shaker writer." He wrote of the "united inheritance" and common life of the Shakers, and explicitly compared it with Catholic monasticism. He viewed the monks with a certain approval for "professing greater sanctity than the Church in general" and for their freedom from marital ties. However, he felt that their dependence on vow instead of "conscience alone" was a weakness, and their reliance on alms led them to be "patronized by public approbation and authority," whereas the Shakers were regarded as outcasts. It is almost certain that Dunlavy must have seen something of the first colony of Trappists established, about this time, only fifty miles from Pleasant Hill, in Nelson County. Unlike the persecuted Shakers, the Trappists were surrounded by the approval and concern of the small Catholic colony, and yet they soon left Kentucky, going to Illinois and then returning to France. They returned to Kentucky to build Gethsemani Abbey in 1848.

The Shakers of Pleasant Hill were harassed and plundered by soldiers of both sides in the Civil War (especially before and after the Battle of Perryville, a few miles away, in the fall of 1862). After the war, vocations began to decline, and in the industrial boom of the late nineteenth century the spiritual and social vigor of the Shakers gradually died out. Since they did not marry, there were no children to carry on the community. A few orphans were adopted, but not all of them took to the Shaker life. Twenty years after the Civil War, registrations ceased at Pleasant Hill and the Family Houses began to close.

As the community dwindled, some members left to consolidate with other communities in the east. The Society at Pleasant Hill was officially dissolved in 1910. A few Shakers remained at Pleasant Hill to conduct a small school. The last Shaker of the Pleasant Hill colony, Sister Mary Settles, a native of Louisville, died there in 1923. For forty years the buildings have been given to other uses or abandoned, but now they are being restored and opened to the public.

After their departure, these innocent people, who had once been so maligned, came to be regretted, loved, and idealized. Too late, the people of Kentucky recognized the extraordinary importance of the spiritual phenomenon that had blossomed out in their midst. Today there is a general

awareness that the Shakers made a unique and original contribution to American culture—but it will take more than nostalgia and sentiment to revive their unique combination of "science, religion and inspiration," which remains to us as a mysterious and fascinating "sign" for our times.

INTRODUCTION TO
Religion in Wood: A Book of Shaker Furniture

Prepare the furniture, O Lambeth, in thy pitying looms!
The curtains, woven tears and sighs, wrought into lovely forms
For comfort: there the secret furniture of Jerusalem's chamber is
*   wrought.*
Lambeth, the Bride, the Lamb's Wife loveth thee:
Thou art one with her, and knowest not of self in thy supreme
*   joy.*
Go on, builders in hope, tho' Jerusalem wanders far away
Without the gate of Los, among the dark Satanic wheels.

William Blake, Jerusalem, *i*

As the work of William Blake comes to be better understood and as the rich store of unpublished Shaker material is studied and brought to light, we will doubtless see that
they have much in common. Blake was, of course, a contemporary of the first Shakers. Though he almost certainly
had nothing to do with them, his *Jerusalem* was written about
the time the Shaker villages were being built in New
England, Ohio, and Kentucky, and the Shaker "style" was
developing in craftsmanship. The Shaker's "religion in
wood" (surely an inspired title) is an expression of a profoundly religious creativity very like that which moved
Blake to write and engrave.

We know now that Blake's apparently wild and hermet-
ic theology is not as incoherent as it was once believed to be,
even though it is not always orthodox! We know also that the
Shakers were something more than a community of

73

eccentrics who had escaped from the world because they could not get along in it. If the Shakers are appreciated today (and in some quarters they are well-loved and their contribution to American culture is rightly evaluated) this is due in part to the work of Edward Deming Andrews who better than anyone else, caught their true spirit, and who interpreted it to the rest of us. This present book is a last and most eloquent word of Dr. Andrews, and in some sense a crowning and summing up of his whole work on Shaker craftsmanship and spirituality. Some time before his death in June 1964, Dr. Andrews had asked me for a preface. As a personal tribute to him I will try, in this meditation on the Shaker aesthetic, to capture something of its deep religious and "monastic" quality. Though it would be easy (as Dr. Andrews himself has shown) to approach them through the Rule of St. Benedict, I have chosen rather to look at the Shakers in the light of the artist and poet, William Blake.

It is no exaggeration to say that the simple and "lovely forms" which emerged from the fire of Shaker religious inspiration had something to do with what Blake called "the secret furniture of Jerusalem's chamber."

Neither the Shakers nor Blake would be disturbed at the thought that a work-a-day bench, cupboard, or table might also and at the same time be furniture in and for heaven: did not Blake protest mightily at the blindness of "single vision" which saw only the outward and material surface of reality, not its inner and spiritual "form" and the still more spiritual "force" from which the form proceeds? These, for Blake,

were not different realities. They are one. And the "fourfold vision" of religious and creative "imagination" (more akin to prophetic vision than to phantasy) was needed if one were to be a "whole man," capable of seeing reality in its totality, and thus dwelling and expanding spiritually in "the four regions of human majesty."

> *Now I a fourfold vision see*
> *And a fourfold vision is given to me;*
> *'Tis fourfold in my supreme delight*
> *And threefold in soft Beulah's night*
> *And twofold always. May God up keep*
> *From single vision and Newton's sleep!*

The Shaker inspiration was communal. The originality of Shaker forms, that is to say the particular development which the craftsmanship of New England and New York in the 18th century underwent in the Shaker milieu, was due not to the individual craftsman but to the community spirit and consciousness of the Believers. It is not only a manifestation of their practicality but a witness to their common faith. Indeed one is tempted to say that it is a better, clearer, more comprehensible expression of their faith than their written theology was. The inspired Shaker simplicity, the reception of simplicity as a charismatic gift, as a sign of truth and of salvation, is powerfully and silently eloquent in the work of their hands.

These men and women, simple, profoundly serious, deeply and religiously vulnerable, open to the winds of change and grace that swept the American frontier, believed that Mother Ann, their foundress, had come from England "with the candle of the Lord in her hand" and with a definitive message. This Shaker message, which has been elaborated in strange and heterodox forms, is nevertheless in its essence deeply Christian. The United Society of Believers in Christ's Second Appearing (the Shakers' official title) were not men of a dour, sulphur-and-brimstone eschatology as one might expect. They were simple, joyous, optimistic people whose joy was rooted in the fact that Christ *had* come, and that the basic Christian experience was the discovery of Christ living in us all now: so that the true Christian is the one who lives and behaves as a "Child of the Resurrection" with his eyes open to a wholly new vision of a redeemed cosmos in which war, hatred, tyranny, and greed had no place— a cosmos of creativity and worship.

In this essentially "monastic" view of life, the duty of the Believer is, as Mother Ann declared, "to labor to make the way of God your own; let it be your inheritance, your treasure, your occupation, your daily calling." This is the first principle of Shaker craftsmanship.

The Believer worked patiently, lovingly, earnestly, until his spirit was satisfied that the work was "just right." Fidelity to the demands of the workman-like conscience was a fundamental act of worship. Through this fidelity, the workman became an instrument of God's loving care for the community. His work was therefore compounded of faith and love and care. It was an expression and fruit of the Shaker covenant. In work, as in worship and in his religious dancing, the Shaker was attuned to the music intoned in each being by God the Creator and by the Lord Jesus.

Work was to be perfect, and a certain relative perfection was by all means within reach: the thing made had to be pre-

cisely what it was supposed to be. It had, so to speak, to fulfill its own vocation. The Shaker cabinetmaker enabled wood to respond to the "call" to become a chest, a table, a chair, a desk. "All things ought to be made according to their order and use," said Joseph Meacham. The work of the craftsman's hands had to be an embodiment of "form." The form had to be an expression of spiritual force. The force sprang directly from the mystery of God through Christ in the Believing artist: the "fourfold vision" of Blake is the key to the religious mystery and luminosity of Shaker craftsmanship. There were of course rules to be obeyed and principles by which the work was guided: but the work itself was free, spontaneous, itself responding to a new and unique situation. Nothing was done by rote or by slavish imitation. The workman also had a vocation: he had to respond to the call of God pointing out to him the opportunity to make a new chest of drawers like the ones that had been made before, only better. Not necessarily better in an ideal and absolute sense, but better adapted to the particular need for which it was required. Thus the craftsman began each new chair as if it were the first chair ever to be made in the world!

One can imagine, then, the Edenic innocence which is the special glory and mystery of Shaker work. Here we admire not the Titanic creativity of the self-conscious genius, aware of a possible mission to disturb and to awaken the world (and perhaps infuriated by his promethean calling). Shakers were not supposed to sign their work, or flaunt trade marks. Their only advertisement was the work itself, and the honesty with which the product was set before the buyer. Above all, the work of the Shakers was made for use rather than for profit (a maxim dear to Eric Gill). This gave it an inimitable honesty which one cannot find in the slick new model of the latest car, tailored like some unearthly reptilian fowl and flashing with pointless gadgetry, marketed to replace other models designed for obsolescence, and to be replaced itself without delay!

The Shaker had his eye not on the market but on the reality of things and on the integrity of life and thought. A Shaker Elder, planting his orchard, remarked: "A tree has its wants and wishes and a man should study them as a teacher watches a child to see what it can do. If you love a plant, take heed to what it likes. You will be repaid by it."

The Shaker's reward was in the response of living beings to his own loving care. The odd Shaker dogma about Christ "reincarnated as a woman" was perhaps not as outlandish in its original meaning as it later came to be. The root idea is that of the "maternal" aspect of God's love, and man's, an aspect too often ignored: the view which sees love as tenderness and care for all living beings (compare the Buddhist meditation on the "four unlimiteds") and indeed for life itself. Such love is one of the deepest forms of respect for the creative tenderness of God whose merciful Spirit of Love broods over all beings.

A Shaker of our own time (there are still two Shaker villages left, one in Maine and one in New Hampshire) has said: "The greatest force in the universe is the love of God . . . and the second greatest is interior prayer." One feels that for the Shaker craftsmen, love of God and love of truth in one's own work came to the same thing, and that work itself was a prayer, a communion with the inmost spiritual reality of things and so with God, not as if the "spirit" of the thing were something distinct from the thing itself, but in a full realization that everything that is, is in a certain sense "spirit," since "spirit," "form," and "actualization" are all one and the same. The Shakers thus had a deeply existential approach to reality.

It has been remarked, and it is worth repeating, that the Shaker vision was peculiarly and authentically American. This is of course a dangerously vague statement, because though there is indeed a very real and very powerful American mystique, it is becoming increasingly difficult to say precisely what it is, since every possible contradiction seems to get included in it (one need only mention the bewilderingly different expressions of freedom and unfreedom which now outdo one another in their claims to be "American"). The Shakers certainly had no political ideology. But they had a well-defined communal organization of their own, based on their religious principles. Unquestionably they felt themselves called to be a force for social renewal in the world which surrounded them. They had the gift to express much that is best in the American spirit. They exemplified the simplicity, the practicality, the earnestness, and the hope that have been associated with the United States. They exemplified these qualities in a mode of humility and dedication which one seeks in vain today in the hubris and exasperation of our country with its enormous power! Mother Ann had a beautiful and Blake-like vision of America, a vision of gentleness and love:

I saw a large tree, every leaf of which shone with a brightness as made it appear like a burning torch . . . I knew that God had a chosen people in America; I saw some of them in vision, and when I met with them in America I knew them.

As Lope de Vega had said earlier (in a different context!): "There is love in the Indies—much more than here!"

Later, some of the Shaker visionaries, the "sensitives" who received inspired subjects for paintings and musical compositions, delighted in painting the "paradise tree." It was of course a peculiarly intense expression of the common hope that in America the earthly paradise had been rediscovered—certainly an essential element in the American mystique. It is interesting to note that in the legendary voyage of the Irish monk St. Brendan (6th century) the Paradise Tree of the New World plays an important and symbolic part. I think, by the way, that this particular symbolic hope needs to be taken seriously precisely in the moment of darkness and deception when in our atmosphere of crisis, bitterness, and confusion, this hope has turned for so many into angry despair and the sacred tree has been stripped of those bright leaves and golden fruits.

Whatever may be the ambiguities and complexities of the American mystique today, let us recall the original

American vocation to be a New World of almost infinite hope, a paradise of refuge, security, peace, growth, and productivity opening its arms to welcome the oppressed, the downtrodden of the "old world." Here especially the religious reformer and the idealist could find a way of realizing hitherto unrealizable hopes. Here utopias could be brought into being and here the Kingdom of God could become an earthly reality. Here the happy citizen, cultivating the rich soil, could live in an innocence and honest joy never to be troubled by intrigues and by the threat of police tyranny, as in the decadent monarchies of Europe. Here were no religious inquisitions. The American was a new being who had nothing to do with the world of European complexity and iniquity. He had only to retain his innocence and keep his "baptismal" robe unsmirched by the dark concerns of Europe the unredeemed.

The Shakers acted out their American conviction within the framework of their own order, well aware that the "world" was very much present around them, and that the serpent had come into paradise. Already the irresponsible waste of mine and forest, of water and land, the destruction of bison and elk, were there to show that Paradise was not indefinitely self-sustaining. Later the doors of the country closed to the immigrant and the refugee. American money became the greatest power in the world, and Paradise realized itself to be surrounded no longer with friendly hope but by impotent environs and frustrated hate.

Unlike Ann Lee's America, ours is, alas, without

angels—perhaps because it is also seemingly without devils. Mother Ann was convinced of the reality of both. She saw the devil and fought with him, and knew he was "a real being, real as a bear." The peculiar grace of a Shaker chair is due to the fact that it was made by someone capable of believing that an angel might come and sit on it. Indeed the Shakers believed their furniture was designed by angels— and Blake believed his ideas for poems and engraving came from heavenly spirits.

This is another way of saying, with Blake, that the creative and religious imagination plays an extremely important part in the life of man, and that an era in which this spiritual imagination is impotent, sterile, or dead, is necessarily going to be an era of violence, chaos, destruction, madness, and slaughter. Describing his own picture of the Last Judgement, Blake wrote:

> *When imagination, art and science and all intellectual gifts, all gifts of the Holy Ghost are looked upon as of no use, and only contention remains to man, then the Last Judgement begins and its vision is seen by the imaginative eye of everyone according to the situation he holds.*

"Imagination," for Blake, is the faculty by which man penetrates ultimate reality and religious mystery. It is completely distinct from "allegorical fantasy."

"I know that this world is a world of imagination and vision [wrote Blake in a letter] . . . but everybody does not see alike. To the eyes of a miser a guinea is more beautiful than the sun, and a bag worn with the use of money has more beautiful proportions than a vine filled with grapes. The tree which moves some to tears of joy is in the eyes of others only a green thing that stands in the way. Some see nature all ridicule and deformity, and by these I shall not regulate my proportions, and some scarce see nature at all. But to the eyes of the man of imagination, nature is imagination itself. As a man is, so he sees. As the eye is formed, so are its powers . . . To me this world is all one continuous vision of fancy or imagination."

Why is the Bible more entertaining and instructive than any other book? Is it not because they [sic] are addressed to the imagination, which is spiritual sensation, and but mediately to the understanding or reason?

Blake's ideas of creative imagination as a necessary medium between man and the reality around him sounds less mad than it used to, since modern science itself (so remote from Blake) has brought us face to face with the fact that the physical constituents of the world around us escape our understanding.

For Blake, as for the Shakers, creative imagination and religious vision were not merely static and contemplative. They were active and dynamic, and imaginative power that did not express itself in creative work could become highly dangerous. So Blake could say,

I know of no other Christianity and no other Gospel than the liberty both of body and mind to exercise the divine arts of imagination, the real and eternal world of which this vegetable

universe is but a faint shadow and in which we shall all live in our eternal imaginative bodies when these vegetable bodies are no more . . . What is the life of man but art and science? . . . Let every Christian as much as in him lies engage himself openly and publically before the world in some mental pursuit for the building up of Jerusalem. A poet, a painter, a musician, an architect: the man or woman who is not one of these is not a Christian . . . The unproductive man is not a Christian, still less the destroyer.

And finally this profoundly just and prophetic view of man's modern plight:

Art degraded, imagination denied, war governed the nations.

The whole history of Shaker craftsmanship and the evidence that has been left to us in the works photographed here cry "Amen" to this doctrine of Blake's. The chastity, the simplicity, the honesty of Shaker work is often praised. Let these pages be a testimony to the unequalled creative imagination of Shaker craftsmanship, which is all the greater because it is never conscious of itself, never seeks recognition, and is completely absorbed in the work to be done.

Shaker craftsmanship is perhaps the last great expression of work in a purely human measure, a witness to the ancient, primitive, perfect totality of man before the final victory of machine technology. A book about such craftsmanship, such wholeness, is inevitably a book with a message. It poses a challenging question: is such a spirit, such work, possible to men whose lives are in full technological, sociological, and spiritual upheaval? Will such a spirit be possible in the future world that will emerge from the present technological revolution, that world whose outlines can barely be discerned? Is Shaker craftsmanship and its spirit necessarily bound up with a more primitive technology, or can it find a way to direct and inform machine production? It is not my business to attempt an answer to a question which, in some ears, would be all but sacrilegious. It is sufficient to add my voice to those who have spoken in this book, with such sincerity and such power of persuasion.

WORK AND THE SHAKERS

A Transcript of a Conference Given by Thomas Merton
at the Abbey of Gethsemani on July 22, 1964

In the Shakers the idea was that you had four or five trades; you just didn't have one trade, you had four or five trades. Some of these early Shakers could do one of any five or six jobs very well—printer, carpenter, cabinetmaker, basket maker. They had five or six things they could do, and if need be, they pitched in and turned out a chair, a table, or a basket, or something like that. This was considered normal, that they had several things that they could do. We don't have to be versatile like that, but it is right in the monastic life that everybody has something that he can do fairly well and within reason, perfectly, and he should get a crack at doing that some of the time, even if it is just a question of sleeping or something like that. Somebody has to be able to do this and to do it well. There should be nobody in the monastery who does not have an opportunity to do some good work because that is part of his life of prayer. So, if you get a person in the monastery who never has a chance to do a decent job of work—all he ever gets to do is frit around and begin something and leave it and pick up something and drop it in the middle—this is fine; it is a great penance but it is not the monastic life, it is not the monastic idea of work. Obviously you are going to get days when you get all messed up and when you can't possibly make any sense out of the work and so forth. This happens. As soon as you get into a big organization like this you are going to get people who are mixed up in useless and fantastic projects. But, as a normal thing, everybody should have something that he really is good at and he really puts his heart into it, he does it, and it is well done and is a part of his life of prayer.

One of the Shakers' chief maxims was "Put your hands to work and your hearts to God." Well, of course, this is normal for us. You work and your heart is lifted up to God while you are working and you are working for God. Now, to work for God means not this business of working and looking at God, but working in such a way that your work is your union with God. Ideally speaking, whatever a person is doing, his work is his union with God. From my own point of view, if I have to write something, if I have to prepare a conference or something like that, the kind of work that is my work—then I have to find God in that work. There is no point in my rushing like mad through a work period and typing fifteen or twenty pages and getting it out by four o'clock and then going to pray. It is not a question of working in a sort of half daze, so you will sort of work and go off a little bit, and come back, and float a little bit, and so forth. It is more a question of when you work, you *think* about your work.

This, I would say, is absolutely fundamental. Don't think that when you are thinking about your work, in so far as it needs to be thought about, it is a distraction. There are certain kinds of work that don't require much thought, so if you don't have to be thinking about the work then okay, then think about anything you want. But still, you have to think enough about the work so the work is going to get done right. But, if you have a job that requires thought, you think about finishing the work right, and that is your prayer.

Some people think this is a sort of an evasion, they say, "You are really getting around the thing, you are not really facing the issue, you are just getting people into a position where they have got to work and not pray. This is a way of getting out of praying." It is not, because if I work properly, with my heart set on the truth of the work, this counts as a prayer because in this I am united with God. Not just that I am doing his will but that I am also seeking him in the truth of what I'm doing.

What you need to remember is the distinction that St. Thomas makes between the *bonum operis* and the *bonum operantis*—*bonum* means good. This gives you some kind of clue as to what making a prayer out of work, by doing the work well, involves. When you are doing anything, you are seeking a good. So, when you are working, the basic thing that you are seeking in your work is a good, the work is good. So the fact of working is good: you are working towards a good, you are seeking a good. Now there is a twofold good that you can seek in a job of work. There is the *bonum operis* and the *bonum operantis*—the good of the work and the good of the worker. What is the difference between those two? What is meant by the good of the work? This is very important. What is the good of the work?

One of the things that one of the Shakers said—it's a beautiful statement—an old fellow was planting an orchard and he was talking about this orchard. "These trees," he said, "you have got to consider what they want, you've got to think about these trees and ask what I would want if I were a tree. Consider their needs and if you consider what the tree wants, when you plant it and take care of it and so forth, you plant it very carefully and beautifully. You consider what the tree wants and you take care of your tree, you give your tree what it wants, and the tree will reward you, the tree will repay you by its response to this treatment." This is a good example of the *bonum operis,* the good of the thing to be made. You take the thing to be made almost as a living reality. If it is a table or a chair or something like that, you consider this almost as a mother considers a child. They would push the idea that far. You are concerned enough about this thing that you are making that this has got to *be*. Here is something that God is calling into *being* through you, and if you pay attention and you take care, this thing is going to have *being*, there is going to be a new *being* in the world which has come into the world through your care and through your love of this *being*. This is a very good way of looking at the thing; this is the way that you look at the good of the work.

The good of the worker—what is the good of the worker? Usually the good of the worker is he sells the thing for ten dollars and he gets his price. That is taking it on the lowest plane. I make the thing, it has a certain price, I sell it for that price, and I get my money and then I go spend the money and then that is it. Now if we are looking at the work purely from the point of view of the *bonum operantis* and the *bonum operantis* is something altogether separate from the work, has nothing to do with the work—if I just simply produce something and I don't care how good it is, providing I can sell it for ten dollars, I'll sell it for ten dollars. If it falls apart immediately, the fellow's got it, why should I worry? Now it's his, and I've got the ten dollars. That is no way to look at work; you can't make work a prayer if you don't consider the *bonum operis*. If I go through the afternoon working and I don't give a hoot what happens, or how it turns out, all I care about is getting to the end of the afternoon so that I can do something else that I want, my afternoon is wasted to

a great extent. I haven't really worked as a monk. It doesn't matter what it is, if it's some small thing and I do the thing really well. For example, I consider something has to be cleaned, and if by the end of the afternoon the thing is cleaned up, and I have wanted to clean it up, fine. It's not a case of I happened to be there and it happened to get cleaned up—this is not a human way of going about it.

What is involved here is the conscience of the worker as

worker, a workman-like conscience. This is a thing that the Shakers stress and that we should develop. It is a conscience that tells you when you are considering the *bonum operis*; you are considering the good to be produced. How does this conscience develop, how are you going to develop a conscience like this? What does it involve? How do you develop any kind of a conscience? Through reflection on what this calls for, what it demands. Somebody asks me to make a table—well, what is a table for? Is it just a flat piece of wood that you can pick up and hold on your knees, or has it got to stand on its own? I think about what it is going to be used for: Is he going to use it for a dinner table? Is he going to use it to keep books on? Is he going to use it to keep his telephone on? What's he going to do with the table? I consider all these things.

You can see when you look at Shaker furniture, which you can do at least in books, that there is a sort of uniformity. They look somewhat alike and yet, nevertheless, there is always a certain amount of individuality in each thing because the man is always making this thing for this particular room and this particular place and this particular time. He is considering it in the light of its relationship with other things, and when you look at things like a chest of drawers that they made, you find there is always some little difference and there is always a reason. The person is always considering this particular situation: this is a brand new situation, this isn't the same situation that I had to work for yesterday, this has to be this way, and they are going to need this here, and so forth. Well that's the thing: if I'm working according to my conscience, a workman-like conscience, I'm thinking in these terms.

Somebody may say, "That's got nothing whatsoever to do with God" but it has a great deal to do with God, because it is concerned with the truth of this work. If I turn out a table that just does not stand up and the first time it is used it collapses—but it's a table, it can be classified as a table, it comes under the genus species of table, but it does none of the things that a table is supposed to do—I haven't considered the truth of the thing. It is not really a true table, it isn't real, it just looks like a table. So, this is very important, and you can apply it to anything; apply it to weeding a garden for example. When you're weeding a garden, to do the thing right, you want to get the weeds out and leave the other things in. If you have weeded a small plot of garden and at the end the things that are out are supposed to be out and the things that are supposed to be in are in, there's a satisfaction there, there's a truth there. It may be a kind of an arbitrary truth; someone may say, "Well, why the heck don't you pull out these morning glories? They're no use to anyone." But if you've got a reason for keeping them, well keep them.

The other maxim that they have is "All things are supposed to be made according to their order and use"—so that a thing is determined by its use, the truth of a thing is determined by its use. Where are we likely to go wrong on something like this? What could be a temptation in regard to having to think about the use of a thing, especially for the choir rather than for the brothers? Consider some material thing,

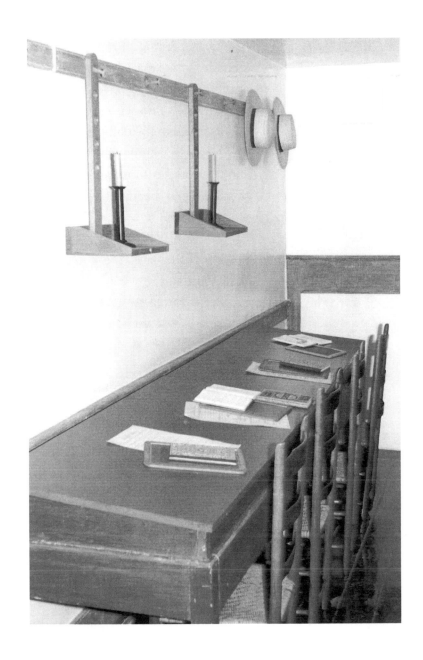

some base, temporal thing. Maybe it has to do with food or something like that. This is a low material occupation, eating stuff is alright, you have got to eat, and so forth. But eating has nothing to do with prayer, and so I throw the bread out and let it fall in the coffee first. "No, a little coffee won't hurt the bread." Things like working in the refectory—what should you be thinking about working in the refectory? What should be the first thing you're thinking about in working in the refectory? That somebody is going to have to eat this stuff; it isn't just that I've got to get it here without dropping it all over the floor. It's nice not to drop it on the floor. Ultimately, what I should be thinking about is that my brother is going to have to eat this. My brother is going to come and sit down here, and he is going to put his elbows on the table—he's going to put them in the strawberries because I got strawberries all over the table which he doesn't see. This is a very important thing, because this makes the thing true, this makes it real, this is a real activity; I have done this for my brother.

Of course, if you push it a little further and you put the religious note into the thing and make it specifically Christian, well, what I've done for my brother I've done for Christ. If I look at it in this sense, when the Day of Judgment comes, this meal that I have put there for this person is a meal that I have served to Christ. This is exactly the way the Shakers looked at this. They looked at it from the point of view of this kind of truth. Therefore, they had this maxim, which is a very good maxim: "Labor until you bring your spirits to feel satisfied." This is a typical Shaker type of thing: we wouldn't think of this so much ourselves. "Labor until you bring your spirits to feel satisfied." What do they mean by that? What are they talking about? Art. Any way of learning how to do the thing right is art. It doesn't have to be a picture or a sculpture or something like that. Art is the right reason for making a thing. So whether it is cooking or whether it is making shoes or sewing a garment or something like that, it is art.

Medicine is an art. If you give a fellow the right pill, it is because of the art. You give a pill that has something to do with what ails this guy. You don't just give him a tranquilizer and hope he'll go to sleep and forget about the whole thing and wake up well. You give him what is going to help him. What's involved here then is a certain inner satisfaction, an inner peace that comes from conforming your mind to the truth that is asked for in the thing outside. He wants his radio fixed; when it is fixed, he turns it on and he gets everything—all the commercials come across great, his radio is fixed. It works, and it continues to work. It doesn't break down again next week, and he's got to come in again and get it fixed all over again. Or he wants his car fixed, and now his car is running. So fine, this is right, so I should feel satisfied. Anybody who does anything, this is a perfectly normal and natural thing, normally speaking likes to get into a situation where he can do the thing and turn it over to the man: "Here, it goes." It works, and it works nice. If a person is really careful about it, he doesn't just fix it, but he fixes it

so it's really good, so you're not going to have trouble with it again for a long time.

This is the way we ought to look at things because this is a natural satisfaction; it is one of the most important natural satisfactions in the monastic life. If you go for days and days and days never getting this kind of satisfaction, you are going to have great problems in your spiritual life. God wants us to live, and this is part of life. This is a very important part of life. One of the sources of trouble about this in the monastery is that all sorts of people have, through one way or another, got a bad conscience on this—their conscience has been badly formed on this. They are afraid to think about the good of the work; they think there is something wrong if you think about the good of the work, that it's a distraction, it's taking their minds away from God. If you're thinking about your work, if you're going to work like this, you're liable to think about it outside the time of work. It doesn't matter, so long as you're not spending whole hours of the office elaborately concocting all the stuff that you're going to do. I mean, don't do that deliberately, but you're bound to think of your work once in a while elsewhere. This is perfectly normal and natural. So, you get a lot of people who would work like this and be very happy with this idea and feel satisfaction with this, but when they go to work, they get this guilty feeling about it, and when they work, they're guilty because they get the idea that work is something that is not contemplative.

On the contrary, this is one of the things that makes the

life contemplative. You can't get a really contemplative life in a monastery if you don't have people working like this. It doesn't mean that everyone has to, but if people on the whole are working like this, the atmosphere of the place is contemplative. It is easier to have a contemplative life where things are done right and things are in good shape and they're in good order, than one where all that is neglected in order to contemplate. That person is not contemplating according to the cenobitic pattern. If he wants to do that, and he can handle it, let him go and live in a cave where there's nothing to do. Let him live in a mess, fine; that's a different vocation. But if he is going to be a contemplative in the community life, he should help everybody to keep things nice because this is important for the community life. It's part of the contemplative life. I think a lot of people are afraid that it isn't; they think contemplation means being on your knees in church and work is non-contemplative—work is action and this other stuff is contemplation, and when you're working you're leading the active life and it's less good and you should feel bad about it, you should want it to stop, you should want to get back to prayer. It is nice to want to pray, but it is also very good for your prayer if you can do your work in this way.

One final thing that the Shakers brought out. The people who were, so to speak, officers in the Shakers were called Elders. One of the qualifications that was looked for in a Shaker Elder was not only that he was a good worker, but that he had gained a gift in his manual labor. Now this means not only was he working well, but he was a person who, through his life of manual labor, had what they would call a special gift. Namely, something like simplicity or humility or something like that. As a result of years of careful work a man would gain a gift. You see, with some of the old brothers around the monastery, they've gained this gift; they have worked and worked and worked, they've broken rocks and taken care of bees and that sort of stuff for years and years and years, and they've gained a gift. They have got a gift of a special kind of humility that you only get from breaking rocks for years and years and years and taking care of bees for years and years. This is a special gift that goes with this kind of work, and other people don't have this gift because they have another gift from other kinds of work.

So therefore the final point is that we should also aim to gain a gift through our work. It should be the gift appropriate to the work. If I'm a writer, I should gain the spiritual gift that goes with being a writer. If I am making fruitcakes, I should get the gift that comes from making fruitcakes. If I'm taking care of this, working in a hotel or something, there should be a gift from that. This is a very important thing because it is one of the spiritual graces of the life; it is one of the things that is really important in the life. Don't let anyone ever fool you on that.

SELECTED CORRESPONDENCE

THOMAS MERTON
TO EDWARD
DEMING ANDREWS

Dear Mr. Andrews:

It was indeed a pleasure to get your kind letter. I had been thinking of writing to you myself for some time, as I know several of your fine books on the Shakers and indeed have the two most important ones here. (I take it that *The People Called Shakers* and *Shaker Furniture* are among your most important studies.) So first of all I want to express my gratitude to you for the fine work you have done and are doing. I shall certainly have to depend very much on you, if I do any work at all in this field, and I am grateful for your offer of assistance.

It is quite true that Shirley Burden and I have discussed the possibility of a book on the Shakers. My part would not be precisely a study of their religion, if by that is to be understood their doctrines, but of their spirit and I might say their mysticism, in practice, as evidenced by their life and their craftsmanship. To me the Shakers are of very great significance, besides being something of a mystery, by their wonderful integration of the spiritual and the physical in their work. There is no question in my mind that one of the finest and most genuine religious expressions of the nineteenth century is in the silent eloquence of Shaker craftsmanship. I am deeply interested in the thought that a hundred years ago our two communities were so close together, so similar, somehow, in ideals, and yet evidently had no contact with one another. I have seen the buildings of the Shaker colony near Harrodsburg here, and of course it speaks volumes to me. There is at present a plan on foot in which you will be interested: some friends of mine in University circles in Lexington are trying to buy the buildings and preserve them in some form or other, perhaps as a study center. If you are interested I can have them get in touch with you, they are having rather a hard time and you might be able to help them. In fact it might be wise eventually to coordinate the various efforts to save the different Shaker communities everywhere. I wrote a little letter to the Shakers at Canterbury N.H. and got a sweet letter back from one of the old ladies, but I have not pursued the correspondence. I ought to try to write to them for Christmas, though.

But in any case, your letter inspires me to pursue further my studies of the Shakers. I will not rush at it and I will try to profit by their example and put into practice some of their careful and honest principles. It would be a crime to treat them superficially, and without the deepest love, reverence and understanding. There can be so much meaning to a study of this kind: meaning for twentieth century America which has lost so much in the last hundred years—lost while seeming to gain. I think the extinction of the Shakers and of their particular kind of spirit is an awful portent. I feel all the more akin to them because our own Order, the Cistercians, originally had the same kind of ideal of honesty, simplicity, good work, for a spiritual motive.

Now I do want to take advantage of your kind offer. I am

still far from getting down to the study I want to do. But if you have any interesting books that are not too precious to lend, which speak of the Shaker spirit in work and living, I would be very happy to borrow them and take care of them. But more urgent than that: I wonder if you could let me have any reproductions of your Shaker inspirational paintings? I would like to use two or three if possible in a book on religious art which is ready for publication.[1] I think certainly some of the trees of life etc would be most suitable (These I have seen in reproduction) but I do not know about the others. Perhaps there is among them something with a special spiritual quality. I would be glad to use anything you can let me have. Of course you will let me know in what terms the acknowledgement should be printed in the book etc. I am very interested in your project to save the Hancock community and shall pray for its success. In fact I pray God to bless all your work and efforts in this regard.

With very cordial good wishes,
Sincerely yours in Christ.

August 22, 1961

Dear Mr. Andrews:

It is a terribly long time since you last wrote and since you sent the little book on the *Millennial Church*. I should have answered you long ago. And I should also have returned the

---

[1]Merton's book on religious art, provisionally entitled "Art and Worship," was never published.

book by this time. I am at last answering and it is in order to accuse myself of slothfulness and lethargy, and ask your indulgence so that I may keep the book a little while longer.

To excuse myself, I can point to the condition of our times, which no one, not even a monk, completely escapes or transcends. I have allowed myself to be involved in more tasks and interests than I should, and the one that has most suffered has been the study of the Shakers. It is in a way so completely out of the theological realm with which I am familiar, although their spirit has so much in common with ours. This makes me hesitant to plunge in deeply, and so I turn to other things in which I feel I can accomplish something. Thus I can tell myself that I have not "wasted time." Yet slow and patient work that does not immediately produce a result is no waste of time . . . I am hoping that I can get back to this kind of study of the Shaker sources later in the fall.

Yet perhaps some of my other interests may remotely cast a light on this study. I am currently very interested in Clement of Alexandria, one of the earliest Christian "gnostics," and his spirit has much in common with that of Shaker simplicity and joy. Then too I am acquainting myself with the magnificent work on primitive religions that has been done by Mircea Eliade. In reality I think he is the one most qualified to give a complete, well rounded appreciation of the Shaker doctrines, practices and spirit. Perhaps some day he will come down here and I will be able to get him interested. It is very certain that the Shakers preserved many

many deeply important religious symbols and lived out some of the most basic religious myths in their Christian and gnostic setting. I cannot help feeling also that the very existence of the Shakers at that particular moment of history has a very special significance, a sort of "prophetic" function in relation to what has come since . . .

Everything regarding Shakers is always of great interest to me. I think often of them, of the extinct colony that was so near here: I think of their simplicity and their mystical fervor. It is always to me a deeply significant thought, and I feel deeply related to them in some kind of obscure communion. I understand that some manuscripts relating to this colony are in the Filson Club in Louisville. I intend to go and look at them. Meanwhile this may attract you to this part of the world. I hope it does.

The copy of the Shaker schoolboy desk which is in our hermitage is a pure joy.

With every best wish, and with the expression of my gratitude and friendship in the Spirit,

Cordially yours.

December 21, 1961

Dear Edward:

Forgive please this very long delay in thanking you for the copy of *Shaker Furniture* which will remain a highly valued possession in the novitiate library.

I believe it is of the highest importance for the novices to see these things, and get used to this wonderful simplicity. This wordless simplicity, in which the works of quiet and holy people speak humbly for themselves. How important that is in our day when we are flooded with a tidal wave of meaningless words: and worse still when in the void of those words the sinister power of hatred and destruction is at work. The Shakers remain as witnesses to the fact that only humility keeps man in communion with truth, and first of all with his own inner truth. This one must know without knowing it, as they did. For as soon as a man becomes aware of "his truth" he lets go of it and embraces an illusion.

I am so glad you liked Clement. If it ever gets printed, I will gladly send you a copy.[2] New Directions is not in a hurry to decide because we are working on a more urgent project, a book of articles against nuclear war.

Speaking of Clement and Alexandria, you know of Philo Judaeus, the Jewish Platonist who flourished in that city. He has a very intriguing book *De Therapeutis* (which I have not yet found and read). In this book he speaks of Jewish monastic communities in Egypt in which there are some similarities with the Shakers. Particularly the fact that they were contemplative communities of men and women, living separately and joining in worship, though separated by a partition. It would seem there might be many interesting facts in this book, and I recommend it to your curiosity. Alexandria remains a fascinating place, and I am sure that more study of the intellectual and spiritual movements that flourished there will prove very rewarding . . .

Very cordially in Christ Our Lord.

September 20, 1962

Dear Edward:

Probably my silence is the result of a more or less fran-

---

[2]*Clement of Alexandria: Selections from the Protreptikos*, an essay and translation by Thomas Merton, was published by New Directions in 1962.

tic effort to preserve some simplicity in my exterior life by only writing letters when I can think about them. Or rather, by trying to convince myself that it is possible to do this when, in reality, it is not possible. So I write business letters under pressure and leave the things I would really like to write until it is too late to write them. Thus I am afflicted with the modern disease, which you perhaps have escaped better than I, although I am supposed to be a monk.

The Gift to Be Simple is a book of inestimable value to me. It has in it so many things that move one by their clarity and truth. The "Gift to be simple" is in fact the "Gift to be true," and what we need most in our life today, personal, national and international, is this truth. Some of the songs are naive, all of them are charming by their honesty, but there is one which contains great power: *Decisive Work.*[3] There is more in this than just a pious song.

I shall continue to enjoy these songs and ponder over them. How beautiful is the Meeting House you have moved over to Hancock. I wish I could be there for its dedication: or at least to see it some time. Perhaps I will.

The story of the Shirley Meeting House is filled with conflict and paradox. At this one need not be surprised,

---

[3]"I have come, / And I've not come in vain. / I have come to sweep / The house of the Lord / Clean, clean, for I've come / And I've not come in vain. / With my broom in my hand, / With my fan and my flail, / This work I will do / And I will not fail, / For lo! I have come / And I've not come in vain." Edward Deming Andrews, *The Gift to Be Simple: Songs, Dances and Rituals of the American Shakers* (New York: Dover Publications, 1940), 60.

because the law of all spiritual life is the law of risk and struggle, and possible failure. There is something significant in the fact that the Shaker ideal was to most people all but impossible, and that therefore it was inevitable that many good men should fall crashing out of the edifice they had helped to build. God alone understands those failures, and knows in what way perhaps they were not failures. Perhaps somewhere in the mystery of Shaker "absolutism" which in many ways appears to be "intolerant" and even arbitrary, there is an underlying gentleness and tolerance and understanding that appears not in words but in life and in work. It is certainly in the songs. Some of us only learn tolerance and understanding after having been intolerant and "absolute." In a word, it is hard to live with a strict and sometimes almost absurd ideal, and the ambivalence involved can be tragic, or salutary. More than anyone else, the Shakers faced that risk and the fruitfulness of their life was a sign of approval upon their daring.

No, I have not settled down to the photo essay. If I did it now, it would be too superficial. I must read and think more. The pictures were taken before any restoration began. I haven't heard much about the progress there, but there does not seem to be a great deal of enthusiasm about it. Let us hope that all will turn out well, worthy of the dear people who left us this monument of truth.

As ever, with the most cordial good wishes to you both in Christ Jesus.

December 28, 1962

Dear Edward:

I was touched at your thoughtfulness in sending me the music for the song "Decisive Work." It is what I would have expected, and I have learned it now, so that I can sing it to myself from time to time when I am alone. I am still deeply convinced that it represents a most important insight into our own time. And of course it is for us in our own way by our faith and obedience to all of God's "words" to attune ourselves to His will and to join in His work, according to our own humble capacities. The Shakers saw this so well, and saw that their work was a cooperation in the same will that framed and governs the cosmos: and more, governs history . . .

With cordial wishes to you both for the New Year, in all friendship, in Christ.

October 29, 1961

THOMAS MERTON
TO RALPH
MCCALLISTER

Dear Mr. McCallister:

I want to take this opportunity to say that I am very pleased at the efforts being made to restore the Pleasant Hill Shaker village. The Shakers and their spirituality seem to me to be extremely significant, as an authentic American form of the Monastic Life, with a Utopian and eschatological cast. The superb and simple products of their craftsmanship are not only eloquent in themselves, but they also speak for the genuine spiritual vitality of the Shakers, and testify to the validity of their ideal, I believe that much is to be done in the

study of the Shaker spirituality in the light of Western and Near Eastern mystical traditions, and also in the light of Jungian depth psychology. Doctrines which were certainly heterodox from a traditional Christian viewpoint, may then assume a special significance in the history of our time. I cannot help feeling that the Shaker movement is something of a mystery that withholds from us, still, a deep significance which may even throw some light on our present predicament in the world. I think this can be said for all the Utopian movements of the nineteenth century, but is especially true of the Shakers. I have as yet no way of substantiating this intuition. Perhaps some day research scholarship may help us to see more clearly into the problem. At any rate, it seems to me that the Pleasant Hill community center can stand as a witness to the vital spiritual forces that were at work in American history of a century ago. Certainly these honest and noble people manifested a very sincere desire to seek the highest truth by the means that they thought most adequate for the purpose. They felt that it was necessary to dedicate their lives completely to their ideal, and they did so without reserve. At a time like the present when we are witnessing the moral disintegration of our society under the pressure of enormous and perhaps demonic forces of the mind, we can ill afford to neglect the simplicity and dedication to truth of these good sincere people who lived up to their belief . . .

Cordially yours in Christ.

January 24, 1962

THOMAS MERTON
TO MARY CHILDS
BLACK

Mary Childs Black:

I need not tell you how I would love to be there on February 2nd.[4] There are few earthly desires I cherish more than the desire to see the Shaker spiritual drawings in the original. I am still hoping that the collection may find its way out here. It is with great regret that I must decline your kind

---

[4]As part of the Abby Aldrich Rockefeller Folk Art Collection's exhibit of Shaker spirit drawings in early 1962, Edward Deming and Faith Andrews were scheduled to take part, on February 2, in a discussion on the influence of religion on American folk art. Mary Childs

invitation. I never obtain permission to travel that far or indeed to travel at all merely for a "social" occasion. This would be called a social occasion, I suppose. Though to me it would be more.

Recently, though, I did have the happiness to get to the old Pleasant Hill Shaker Community near here, and even took some photographs which came out quite well and I hope I will be able to use them in a little photo essay on the place and on the Shakers. The ideas have not crystallized out yet, and one must give them time. I know Edward Andrews will be interested, though.

This much I can do: share with you all a few thoughts that are at work in my mind about the Shakers and their deep significance, which manifests itself in a hidden and archetypal way in their art, craftsmanship and in all their works. Their spirit is perhaps the most authentic expression of the primitive American "mystery" or "myth": the paradise myth. The New World, the World of renewal, of return to simplicity, to the innocence of Adam, the recovery of the primeval cosmic simplicity, the reduction of divisions, the restoration of unity. But not just a return to the beginning, it is also an anticipation of the end. The anticipation of eschatological fulfillment, of completion, the New World was an earnest and a type of the New Spiritual Creation.

Black's first letter to Merton contained an invitation to him to attend the seminar, as "no one is better able to understand this form of folk art filled with mystery and mysticism." Mary Childs Black to Thomas Merton, January 23, 1962.

In the secular realm this consciousness was of course very pronounced, the consciousness of the pioneer and later of the businessman who thought that America could literally be the earthly paradise. The belief that there was nothing impossible, that all goodness and all happiness was there for the asking. And in the poor of other lands, America existed as the place where they thought gold could be picked up on the streets.

For the Shakers, it was a different consciousness, for at the same time they saw the deceptiveness of the secular hope, and their eyes were open, in childlike innocence, to the evil, the violence, the unscrupulousness that too often underlay the secular vision of the earthly paradise. It was a paradise in which the Indian had been slaughtered and the Negro was enslaved. In which the immigrant was treated as an inferior being, and in which he had to work very hard for the "gold" that was to be "picked up in the streets."

The Shakers realized that to enter into a genuine contact with the reality of the "paradise spirit" which existed in the wonderful new world, they had to undergo a special kind of conversion. And their conversion had this special, unique, wonderful quality in that it, more than any other "spirit," grasped the unique substance of the American paradise myth, and embodied it in a wonderful expression. For myths are realities, and they themselves open into deeper realms. The Shakers apprehended something totally original about the spirit and the vocation of America. This has remained hidden to everyone else. The sobering thing is that their vision was eschatological! And they themselves ended.

BIBLIOGRAPHY

Andrews, Edward Deming. *The Gift to Be Simple: Songs, Dances and Rituals of the American Shakers.* New York: Dover Publications, 1940.

———. *The People Called Shakers.* New York: Oxford University Press, 1953.

Andrews, Edward Deming, and Faith Andrews. *Fruits of the Shaker Tree of Life: Memoirs of Fifty Years of Collecting and Research.* Stockbridge, MA: Berkshire Traveller Press, 1975.

———. *Religion in Wood: A Book of Shaker Furniture.* Bloomington: Indiana University Press, 1973.

———. *Shaker Furniture: The Craftmanship of an American Sect.* New York: Dover publications, 1950.

Dickens, Charles. *American Notes for General Circulation.* Harmondsworth, UK: Penguin, 1972.

Higgins, Michael. "Monasticism as Rebellion: The Blakean Roots of Merton's Thought." *American Benedictine Review* 39:2 (June 1988): 178-87.

Merton, Thomas. *Ascetical and Mystical Theology: An Introduction to Christian Mysticism (From the Apostolic Fathers to the Council of Trent).* Mimeographed copy of lectures given at the Abbey of Gethsemani in the archives of the Thomas Merton Center, Bellarmine University, Louisville, Kentucky.

———. *The Courage for Truth: The Letters of Thomas Merton to Writers.* Selected and edited by Christine M. Bochen. New York: Farrar, Straus and Giroux, 1993.

———. *Dancing in the Water of Life: Seeking Peace at the Hermitage.* Edited by Robert E. Daggy. San Francisco: HarperCollins, 1997.

———. "Introduction" to *Religion in Wood: A Book of Shaker Furniture*, by Edward Deming Andrews and Faith Andrews. Bloomington: Indiana University Press, 1973: vii-xv.

———. *Mystics and Zen Masters*. New York: The Noonday Press, 1988.

———. *Natural Contemplation*. Kansas City: Credence Cassettes, 1987.

———. *New Seeds of Contemplation*. New York: New Directions, 1961.

———. *The Other Side of the Mountain: The End of the Journey*. Edited by Patrick Hart. San Francisco: HarperCollins, 1998.

———. *Raids on the Unspeakable*. New York: New Directions, 1966.

———. *A Search for Solitude: Pursuing the Monk's True Life*. Edited by Lawrence S. Cunningham. San Francisco: HarperCollins, 1996.

———. *The Seven Storey Mountain*. London: Sheldon Press, 1975.

———. "The Shakers: American Celibates and Craftsmen Who Danced in the Glory of God." *Jubilee* 11 (January 1964): 36-41.

———. *Turning toward the World: The Pivotal Years*. Edited by Victor A. Kramer. San Francisco: HarperCollins, 1996.

———. *A Vow of Conversation*. Basingstoke, Hants., UK: Lamp Press, 1988.

———. *The Waters of Siloe*. New York: Harcourt Brace and Company, 1949.

The Rule of St. Benedict for Monasteries. Translated by Dom Bernard Basil Bolton. N.p., 1969.

Skees, Suzanne. *God among the Shakers: A Search for Stillness and Faith at Sabbathday Lake*. New York: Hyperion, 1998.

Photographs by Thomas Merton were taken at Pleasant Hill, Kentucky.

Photographs by Paul Pearson were taken at the following: Hancock, Massachusetts (39, 51, 102); Pleasant Hill, Kentucky (20, 64, 68, 78, 119); South Union, Kentucky (36, 47, 57, 99, 112).